The Homemade Coffee Cookbook

From Beginner to Home-Barista:
200+ Coffee Recipes with Pro Tips to
Make the Perfect Mocha, Cappuccino,
Espresso Drinks, White, Cocktails & Iced
Coffee and More!

Vincent D'Angelo

Table of Contents

DOWNLOAD THE FILE WITH
COLOR IMAGES FOR FREE!

"Dear Reader,

Since we do not consider a cookbook with non-color images to be worthy., we have chosen not to include images of the dishes for this kindle version.

But don't worry!

To thank you for your purchase, we decided to give you the PDF version of this book for free, with all the images of the recipes described in color!

This way, you have the ability to access this cookbook at any time from any device.

Download the file for free by using this QR Code:

Enjoy reading!"

Vincent D'Angelo

Introduction

I love coffee. And since you've picked up this book for yourself, I think it's a pretty accurate assumption that you love coffee too. Cappuccino, mocha, espresso, iced coffee—these are all things that we can order at our local Starbucks. But these days we all want to know exactly what is going into our bodies through what we consume. Many of us cook our own food just fine, but the most we can do when it comes to coffee is a simple brew with store bought ingredients, pre-packaged grounds, or even just instant coffee.

You might have even thought about growing, roasting and grinding your own coffee, but there's just so many different factors to consider and so much work that goes into it.

That's why I'm here. In this book, I will start off by giving you a brief but comprehensive guide on how to grow and roast your own coffee from scratch; before we get into the main attraction, which is all the amazing recipes that you can go on to make with said coffee. Trust me, there's something magical about drinking coffee that you made with your own two hands, hard work, patience, and love. Of course, even if you don't use home grown coffee, these recipes will still be the highlight of any day.

So before we get into the recipes, let's start with that little guide on how to grow your own coffee from bean to, well, bean.

Cultivating

Firstly, let's go through some useful information.

- I do have to warn you, it takes a long time to actually see the (literal) fruits of your labor. The average coffee tree takes between three and five years to produce its first fruit. Don't let this put you off growing your own coffee trees. It will be worth it when you're drinking that perfect cup of coffee that you were 100% responsible for.
- If you're not willing to wait so long, you could always buy a young coffee plant from a nursery and transplant it in your house or garden. This will reduce the amount of time before the first flowering, but it will likely still be some time before you can actually pick the coffee—unless you buy a fully grown tree that has already started producing fruit.

- The most commonly drunk coffee is made from the Arabica coffee plant. It's also the most beginner-friendly, so the entire planting and caring sections are going to focus only on the arabica tree. The other types of coffee need entirely different care.
- Coffee plants are green, leafy, and really pretty, so they make nice house plants. You just need to make sure that you trim them often to avoid them getting too big. They can grow up to 15 feet; they are trees, after all.
- They should not be near any cool breezes as it can cause them to shrivel. So don't put them near an open window on a windy day or under an air conditioner.
- **Very important!** Keep in mind that apart from the fruit (the coffee cherry), every part of a coffee plant is toxic to both humans and animals. It's not deadly, but it can make people and pets very sick, so keep the plant somewhere where your kids or furry friends can't get to them.

Now that that's out of the way, let's move on to the long but satisfying process of growing your own coffee plant.

Where to Plant a Coffee Tree

First and foremost, where should you plant your coffee tree? Indoors? Outdoors? In the sun? In the shade? There's a couple of factors to keep in mind when deciding where to plant your new friend.

Coffee is a tropical plant and it thrives in hot, humid weather. Therefore, if you live in a country with a cold climate, you would be better off either keeping it inside as a houseplant, or in a temperature regulated greenhouse. Obviously, since it's a tropical plant, it will grow better and have less to tend to if you live in a tropical climate.

The second thing to consider is that, even though coffee plants love the heat, they aren't fans of direct sunlight (yeah, they're fussy little things) so if you plant them outside, make sure it's not in an area that gets a whole lot of exposure to the blazing sun. In a bit of irony, if you keep the plants inside, they thrive if they're put near a sunny window. So, they do like the sun, they just don't like all those UV rays that come with it.

How to Plant a Coffee Tree

As with any plant, the soil you plant it in is incredibly important. Ideally, your soil must have a medium acidity level (around pH 6 is fine) and must be a well draining soil instead of something heavy and dense like clay. The best soil to use for coffee trees is loam, which is a mixture of sand, silt, and clay. You can typically get loam at any hardware or gardening specialty stores. If you can't find loam, you can try using any kind of light, highly porous soil instead. To make sure that the water drains well (which is very important later on), you can add a layer of rocks, followed by a layer of smaller stones before adding the soil on top. This step is not really necessary, but it will help you to be sure that the water will drain completely instead of sitting at the bottom of the pot, soaking the soil—as doing so can cause problems for your plant. To your soil, add manure, bone meal, or other specialized nutrients that you can get from your nursery. Getting the soil to be just right will be a lot more difficult if you're planting it outside in soil that's naturally in the ground. Thankfully, you don't have to worry about drainage as much as you would if you planted it in a pot (although, the more porous the soil, the better, but don't worry too much if your soil isn't perfect), just make sure that the pH level is low and that you add the manure, bone meal and other nutrients like if you were to plant it in a pot. But be sure to ask the experts at your gardening store before putting chemicals on your soil. If it is too alkaline, aluminum sulfate, sulfur, and certain composts can lower your soil's pH level.

Once your soil is sorted out, it's time to move on to the main star of the show: the coffee beans themselves. In order to plant a coffee tree, you're going to need green coffee beans, which are also the seeds of the plant. You can find these in gardening stores in their ready-to-plant state, or you could get them from ripe, freshly harvested coffee cherries (we'll talk a bit more about coffee cherries and how to get the beans out of them later).

It's recommended that you plant a few beans and not just one, as you don't know which ones will germinate. So, take a few beans, place them in a small bowl filled with water, and soak them for about a day. Once they've been fully soaked, there are a few ways you can begin the germination process:

- Place the beans spread out evenly in between two small burlap sacks, pre-moistened with water. Place the sacks near a window and make sure to keep them damp over the next few days or weeks.

- You could also place them inside very shallow, wet, soil; either in the ground, or in a small container. Again, make sure to keep the soil wet.

- Vermiculite, a type of porous mineral, can also be used. You would use it just as you would soil. Make sure it's shallow and keep it well-moistened.

Germination

After a few days or weeks (depending on your climate and the quality of the bean), you should be able to see some little green sprouts poking up and leaning toward the sun. This is the end of the *successful* germination process and you can now move on to planting the little coffee sprouts in a bigger pot. You can plant them directly into a big pot, or you could plant the sprouts in a small pot and let them grow there for the first few months (this is my recommendation), until the plant becomes strong and develops its roots, and *then* transplant it into the bigger pot.

If your ultimate goal is to plant the trees in the ground outside, I would still recommend planting them in a small pot first, at least until they begin to get a bit stronger and more resilient. Especially if you have heavy rains or winds. Little sprouts might not survive harsh weather, so just to be safe, keep them in a small pot on a windowsill, or outside in a shady area (unless the weather is bad, of course).

The method of actually planting the sprouts into a pot is very easy. If you're using soil or vermiculite, simply dig a shallow hole in the target pot's soil, take the sprouts with the soil they're planted in and transfer it to the new pot. In the case of a coffee sack, unless you have a biodegradable one, you're going to have to carefully remove each sprout and replant them in small, shallow holes inside the pot, making sure that the bean and any forming roots are under the soil. Make sure to be very light handed with the soil and don't pack it too much as doing so could damage the sprout or lead to inadequate water drainage.

Water it daily, but don't flood it. You want to keep the soil damp and moist, but not soaking wet. After a while, you'll begin to notice actual leaves growing. There will be small leaves at first, but over time they will get bigger and the plant itself will become more sturdy. If you've planted them in small pots first, this would be the time to transfer them to their ultimate destination, whether that's inside or outside.

Using a gardening trowel, make a hole in your soil, about as wide as the small pot, and deep enough to fit all the soil that the plant is currently occupying. Also with a trowel, carefully dig around the edges of the soil in the small pot and try to take out all of the soil—along with the plant—in one chunk. Place it inside the hole you made in the bigger pot or the ground. Even out the soil (remember not to pack it too much), water it, and voila! Your coffee plant is on it's way to the rest of its beautiful life.

Caring for Your Plant

Once your plant is finding its roots, you can start watering it less often. Depending on the weather and whether you decide to keep it inside or outside, how often you water the plant will change. If you keep it inside, you may only have to water it once a week, but if it's outside, it could dry up much quicker, so you might even have to keep watering it daily. The basic rule is that you have to strive to keep the soil moist, not wet, and definitely do not let it dry out.

Make sure that there's no standing water touching your soil or plant. If you're keeping it in a pot, check the tray often to make sure that it's not full of water. You will likely find some water in the tray, especially if you use a good draining soil, but it shouldn't be excessive amounts. If you find a lot of water, then you're most likely over watering your plant. A little bit of water can go a long way.

As I mentioned before, coffee trees are fussy when it comes to the sun, so remember to keep them somewhere sunny—but not too sunny. If you've planted them outside, try covering them with something that lets only a bit of light in, like a tinted shade or solid structure with a few holes in it. Think of it this way, coffee trees are understory plants; essentially meaning that, in their natural habitat, they grow under the canopy of other trees, so the only sun they get is what shines through the other trees. Try your best to emulate that.

Keep the plants warm and use a fertilizer on the soil every two to three months. Avoid using fertilizer in winter as winter is the plant's 'resting' time, so let the poor guy relax for a few months.

Common Problems and Their Solutions

Problem: The leaves are starting to look droopy and sad.

Solution: The poor plant is thirsty. Most of the time when the leaves droop, it's because it doesn't have enough water. They should go back to normal within a few hours after getting the adequate amount of water.

Problem: The leaves are falling off.

Solution: This is the opposite problem from the previous one. This time, the plant has too much water and the roots may be beginning to rot. Make sure not to over water it, that the soil is well draining, and that it's not sitting in a puddle of water.

Problem: The leaves are turning brown.

Solution: Chances are, they're getting just a bit too much sun. Remember how picky they are about the sun? If they start browning, try moving them to a less sunny spot or placing a shade over them.

Harvesting

How to Harvest the Coffee

As I mentioned earlier, it can take anywhere from three to five years for you to finally see the first flowers on your coffee tree, but once you do, get excited. That means you're going to be able to drink home grown coffee soon and that all your patience was worth it!

A little while after they flower, the tree will produce a bunch of little fruit that looks like berries. We call these coffee cherries. They will start off green and eventually ripen into a deep red color, at which point they are ready for harvesting. Unfortunately, like most fruit trees, not all of the cherries ripen at the same time, so if your tree only produces a handful of cherries, chances are you might only be able to pick a few at a time (i.e. not enough for that perfect cup of coffee that you've been so looking forward to). If that does happen and you have the time and patience for it, I would recommend harvesting, processing, and roasting the cherries as they ripen instead of all at once. It will take more than one processing period (which is a bit long already), but eventually, you'll have the coffee you need. Don't let the cherries over ripen and, while some people do pick them while they're green, it's best to wait until they're at least a little red.

When you're happy with the ripeness, you can go ahead and pick the cherries. Some people like to go through their trees and only hand pick all of the fully ripe ones. Generally, this is how they do it in the coffee fields for premium coffees, but it is also labor intensive—especially if you have many trees and a lot of fruit. The other method that you could consider is something called strip picking, which is where you strip an entire branch of its fruit at once, regardless of whether all of them are ripe or not. It's really up to you to decide which method you use.

With all the cherries now picked, you need to start working on getting to that bean inside as soon as possible. Coffee cherries are still fruit, so they can begin to go bad or get moldy rather quickly, especially in the warmer months. Don't keep them for too long before starting the processing phase.

The Process of Processing

The first step of processing is to get rid of that beautiful fruit you just spent so long picking. Well, getting rid of the outer layer that is. Remember, our goal is to get to the bean—or the seed—in the middle of the fruit. The easiest way to do this is, quite obviously, with some sort of specialized equipment, but the majority of us don't exactly have access to coffee processing machines at home. Not to worry though, there are many other ways of doing it that work just as well but are a bit more time and labor intensive.

- You could go in and remove each one by hand, squeezing and peeling until you reach the bean. You could use a knife to cut away at the flesh of the fruit too, but just be careful not to damage the center where the bean is.

- Another way is to place some of the fruit between two pieces of wood and lightly grind them in a circular motion until the majority of the fruit detaches from the seed. You could even do this one at a time if it's easier for you.

- The third way is to place a bunch of cherries into a bowl or a bucket and tamp them with something wooden until they separate. Essentially, you just have to press down and grind them lightly, kind of like what you would do with a mortar and pestle, but not as strongly. You're just trying to get rid of the top layer of fruit, you're not trying to grind it into powder. This process will separate the fruit from the seed and you can then either hand pick each of the beans or fill the bowl with water and get rid of the pieces of fruit that will likely float up to the top.

- Be creative and come up with your own preferred method of removing the bean from the fruit.

Whichever way you choose to do it, you now have (hopefully) an entire bowl of unprocessed coffee beans.

The next step is to soak those beans in water for around 24 hours. We do this in order to remove the layer of mucilage (that's that slimy stuff that's clinging onto the seed at the moment). This soaking process can take anywhere from 16 to 48 hours, but 24 hours is usually long enough.

After a day has passed, check if they're ready by taking out one bean and rinsing it well. If it still feels a bit slick or slippery, then it needs to stay in the water for another few hours. If it feels rough and almost squeaky clean, then it's ready for the next step. Rinse out the rest of the beans roughly, making sure to get all of that mucilage out. You should rinse them three to four times or until the water runs clear, as if you were removing the starch from rice.

Once they're all nice and clean and mucilage free, it's time to dry them.

You could use a dehydrator for this step if you would prefer. Dehydrate them at around 104° F or 40° C.

The more common way to do this is to sun dry the beans. Spread them out on trays or a large tarp and place them outside to dry in the sun for a few days. Be wary of any rain and, if your area gets a lot of dew or mist, you may want to consider bringing them inside at night and only putting them out during the sunniest parts of the day. The entire drying process can take anywhere from five days to an entire month—depending on the climate—so keep an eye on them. When they are sufficiently dry, you'll notice the outer layer becomes pale, flaky, and brittle. This outer layer is called the parchment.

You now need to move on to the hulling phase, which is just removing the layer of parchment from the beans. You can do so by placing a handful of beans into a container, seal the lid shut, and then shake the beans vigorously until the parchment flakes off. Alternatively, you could place a handful of beans inside a hessian bag and rub them together until the parchment detaches. Like the process of removing the fruit, you can be creative about this step too. Either way, you then dust off all the parchment particles from your beans and you now have beautiful green coffee beans, ready for roasting or replanting.

Roasting

Let's look at two different ways that you can roast coffee beans at home. Of course, you could always use a specialized coffee roaster, in which case you will have to follow the instructions of that specific machine. The methods listed here are ones you can do at home for a fraction of the price of a fancy coffee roasting machine. Let's get right into it.

Oven Roasted

When you roast coffee with any method, the first thing you must always make sure to do is ventilate the area that you will be working in. Ventilate it *well*. When coffee roasts, it gets extremely smoky, so turn on any fans and extractors you may have before you begin, to avoid being smoked out of your own house.

So, once you're satisfied that you won't asphyxiate, get out a large, flat roasting pan. Ideally, you should use a perforated pan (that's the ones with all the little holes in the pan for more even roasting), but you can use any pan that you prefer.

Preheat your oven to around 500° F. Yes, that hot. You're only going to be roasting the beans for a maximum of eight minutes, so it has to be hot enough to rapidly toast them.

Spread the beans in an even, single layer over the bottom of the pan and place it in the oven, preferably on the middle shelf because that's the spot that has the most even temperature throughout. Leave this to roast, shaking the pan periodically (make sure you wear some good quality oven mitts, you don't want to be burned by a 500 degree oven).

After about four to five minutes, the beans will be lightly roasted. Some people like to use lightly roasted beans for their coffee, but the majority of people prefer it to be medium. If you have some beans to spare, try using them in their lightly roasted state and see what you think. You never know, you might find that you prefer it to a medium roasted bean.

If you do want to go all the way to medium, then leave them in the oven for a further two minutes (so, for a total of six to seven minutes). You'll be left with that beautiful dark brown bean that we see in every coffee ad. Not to mention, as long as your area is well ventilated and you're not being overcome with smoke, you should be basking in the delicious coffee smell right about now too. Big plus.

Take the tray out of the oven quickly as coffee can burn really easily and the last thing you want after all that hard word is burnt coffee. You now need to cool it down as quickly as possible, since they're perfectly cooked and you don't want them to overcook. Carefully throw the hot beans into a metal colander and—again—*carefully* toss until they are cool.

Once everything has calmed down and is sufficiently cooler, you unfortunately still have to wait for that amazing cup of coffee. After roasting, the beans release gasses and you have to wait around 12 hours for that to dissipate completely before you grind them. So spread them out on a flat surface and allow them to do their thing.

Roasted With a Popcorn Maker

Yes, those little automatic popcorn poppers can be used to roast coffee. However, it is incredibly important to be super careful with these. There is a high potential for burning yourself if you use the wrong machine, so I would highly recommend looking up online which models are best for coffee bean roasting and going with others' past experiences. The reason for this is that many popcorn makers jostle the seeds to evenly heat them, so there's a chance that hot coffee beans could end up flying everywhere if you're not careful. That's not to discourage you from using this method, I'm just telling you that you need to be safety conscious.

Once again, the first step is to make sure that the place is very well ventilated so that smoke doesn't fill up your house.

Preheat the machine for a minute or two and then add in the coffee. Many popcorn makers come with a little cup that fills up just the right amount of popcorn for the machine; add the same amount of coffee as you would popcorn. If you don't have one of these, there's usually some kind of indication in the instructions or on the machine itself telling you how much popcorn to use. Simply add that amount of coffee, instead.

Once the coffee is in, attach the lid quickly and allow it to jostle and roast the beans. You'll likely get a lot of little particles (chaff) coming out, so try to make sure that it's somewhat contained and not making your kitchen incredibly dirty.

Because all popcorn makers are different, the time it takes to roast the beans will differ, so you have to use the color and the smell of the beans to determine when they're done to your preference. Unfortunately, this can only be achieved through trial and error, but it's usually no less than five minutes and no more than ten.

Once the beans are sufficiently roasted, place them in the metal colander and toss to cool, then leave them to degas for at least 12 hours.

Feel free to experiment with roasting until you find a method that works best for you. You could use a frying pan on a stove or even a sheet pan on a grill, just be sure to take the necessary safety precautions whenever you try something new.

Grinding

Now that you finally have the perfectly roasted beans that you've been waiting so long for, it's time for the final step: grinding them for use.

Like the roasting step, this is, of course, much quicker and easier if you have a specialized coffee grinder, but there are alternate ways to grind your coffee. Some of them are more effective than others and it all depends on what equipment you have on hand (although the most effective would obviously be the coffee grinder).

Blender

Some blenders have a specific setting to grind coffee beans, so if you're lucky enough to have one of those on hand, then go ahead and use it according to the manual. If it doesn't have that setting, don't stress, you can still grind the coffee with a regular, albeit powerful, blender.

Add just a handful of beans to the blender and pulse for three to five seconds at a time until they're sufficiently ground. If the coffee is not grinding evenly, you could tilt or shake the blender between pulses. Be careful not to do this for too long or you could risk making the beans bitter.

Rolling Pin and Plastic Bag

This method (along with the next two methods) requires some good old fashioned upper body strength. All you need is a large rolling pin, a ziploc bag or any equivalent, and a strong, sturdy surface.

Place a good amount of beans into the bag—the amount will differ depending on the size of the bag—and place the rolling pin on top. Methodically press down over different sections of the bag to crack the beans, then roll it back and forth over the entire bag, occasionally shaking it to even everything out until everything is ground to your preference.

Mortar and Pestle

This is not as physically demanding as using the rolling pin, but you'll likely only be able to grind a small amount of beans at a time, depending on the size of your mortar and pestle, so it may take longer. Most of us have a small set for muddling or grinding spices, but if you have a large one, then this might be your preferred method.

Simply fill around one quarter of the mortar with the coffee beans, then press down and twist with the pestle. Some people find it easier to hold the mortar in their other hand while grinding, while others prefer to place it down on a sturdy surface, so just see what feels better for you. Continue doing this until you achieve the desired consistency.

First thing's first, you are not going to be beating the coffee beans with a hammer, as therapeutic as that might sound. Instead, you're going to use your hammer or other heavy object to press down firmly on the beans, gently cracking them, similar to the rolling pin method.

Place the beans in a ziploc bag and methodically press down with your object of choice until the beans are ground, periodically shaking the bag to ensure that everything is even. This method might leave you with kind of a rough, uneven grind, so it's not really the first method I would encourage you to try, but if all else fails, give it a shot.

Coffee

And now… finally, after literal years of blood, sweat and tears, you have the perfect home grown, home roasted, and home ground coffee that is going to change your life forever.

I'm going to stop being dramatic, but still, congratulations! You made your own coffee! It's time to celebrate by brewing that amazing cup and enjoying the fruits of your labor. But don't go anywhere just yet! Why not try one of the delicious recipes coming up with that fresh batch of coffee you just ground? I promise you won't regret it!

Chapter 1. MOCHA

1. The Simple Mocha

Preparation time: 5 minutes
Cooking time: 5 minutes
Servings: 1

Ingredients:

- 1 1/4 cups 2% milk
- 2 tbsp chocolate syrup
- 1 (1.5 fluid oz.) jigger brewed espresso
- 1 tbsp sweetened whipped cream (optional)

Directions:

1. Add milk and heat to 145-165 F with the steaming wand in a steaming pitcher. In a large coffee mug, measure chocolate syrup.
2. Brew espresso, then pour it into the cup. Add steamed milk to the cup, and use a spoon to hold back the foam. Place whipped cream on top.

Nutrition: Calories: 266, Carbohydrate: 39.1 g, Fat: 7.2 g, Protein: 11 g

2. Mocha Smoothies - Hazelnut

Preparation time: 10 minutes
Cooking time: 0 minutes
Servings: 3

Ingredients:

- 1 cup whole milk
- 4 tsp espresso powder
- 2 cups vanilla ice cream
- 1/2 cup Nutella
- 6 ice cubes
- Chocolate curls, as you like (optional)

Directions:

1. Combine the espresso powder, Nutella, and milk in a blender. Cover and process till blended. Place in ice cubes, then cover; blend till smooth.
2. Add ice cream, then cover; blend till smooth. Transfer into chilled glasses. Serve with chocolate curls as garnish if preferred.

Nutrition: Calories: 474, Carbohydrate: 55 g, Fat: 27 g, Protein: 9 g

3. Mocha Drink with Cookies & Cream

Preparation time: 15 minutes
Cooking time: 0 minutes
Servings: 2

Ingredients:

- 2 scoops cookies n crème ice cream
- ½ cup iced mocha coffee
- Whipped cream (for topping)
- 2 cookie n crème sandwich biscuits (crushed for topping)

Directions:

1. Add the ice cream and iced mocha coffee to a blender. Blitz until smooth.
2. Pour into a tall glass and swirl whipped cream on top. Sprinkle over the crushed cookies and serve!

Nutrition: Calories: 200, Carbs: 27g, Fat: 9g, Protein: 3g

4. Mexican Iced Mocha

Preparation time: 5 minutes
Cooking time: 0 minutes
Servings: 1

Ingredients:

- 4 oz. whole milk
- 1 tbsp. chocolate syrup, or to taste
- 1 dash of hot pepper sauce
- ice cubes, as needed
- 4 oz. cold brew coffee

Directions:

1. Combine the hot sauce, chocolate syrup, and milk in a glass, then thoroughly stir till mixed.
2. Add ice, then pour over ice with cold brew concentrate in a second glass. Stir in the milk chocolate-chilly mixture till combined.

Nutrition: Calories: 130, Carbohydrate: 19.3 g, Fat: 3.9 g, Protein: 4.1 g

5. White Chocolate Mocha

Preparation time: 5 minutes
Cooking time: 0 minutes
Servings: 2

Ingredients:

- 1 1/4 cups 2% milk
- 2 tbsp white chocolate-flavored syrup
- 1 (1.5 fluid oz.) jigger brewed espresso
- 1 tbsp sweetened whipped cream

Directions:

1. Add milk and heat to 145-165 F with the steaming wand in a steaming pitcher.
2. In a big coffee mug, measure white chocolate syrup.
3. Pour the brewed into your mug, and add the steamed milk in the mug; hold back the foam with a spoon. Add whipped cream on top. Serve.

Nutrition: Calories: 269, Carbohydrate: 41.6 g, Fat: 6.8 g, Protein: 10.2 g

6. Mocha – Iced Cola

Preparation time: 5 minutes
Cooking time: 0 minutes
Servings: 1

Ingredients:

- ice, as needed
- 1 tbsp coffee granules
- 1 ½ fluid oz. half-and-half
- 1 (12 oz.) can cola-flavored carbonated beverage

Directions:

1. Fill ice in a pretty tall glass, put in the coffee granules
2. Gradually add cola to the glass.
3. Stir half-and-half into the cola. Serve and enjoy!

Nutrition: Calories: 217, Carbohydrate: 41.5 g, Fat: 5.2 g, Protein: 1.6 g

7. Icy Mocha Drink

Preparation time: 5 minutes
Cooking time: 0 minutes
Servings: 4

Ingredients:

- 1 cup milk
- 2 tbsp coffee granules
- 1 tsp vanilla extract
- 3 tbsp instant chocolate drink mix
- 2 tbsp honey
- 14 to 16 ice cubes

Directions:

1. Combine all the ingredients in a blender. Cover and process the mixture until smooth.
2. Pour it into the chilled glasses to serve.

Nutrition: Calories: 143, Carbohydrate: 30 g, Fat: 3 g, Protein: 3 g

8. Mocha Coffee - Cinnamon

Preparation time: 5 minutes
Cooking time: 10 minutes
Servings: 6

Ingredients:

- 1/2 cup ground dark roast coffee
- 1/4 tsp ground nutmeg
- 1 cup 2% milk
- 1/4 cup packed brown sugar
- Whipped cream, optional
- 1 tbsp ground cinnamon
- 5 cups water
- 1/3 cup chocolate syrup
- 1 tsp vanilla extract

Directions:

1. Combine the nutmeg, cinnamon, and coffee grounds in a small bowl. Pour into a drip coffeemaker's coffee filter. Add water and follow to manufacturer's directions to brew.
2. Combine brown sugar, chocolate syrup, plus milk in a big saucepan. Cook while occasionally stirring over low heat till sugar dissolves.
3. Add in brewed coffee and vanilla; stir. Transfer into mugs; add whipped cream to garnish if preferred.

Nutrition: Calories: 126, Carbohydrate: 25 g, Fat: 2 g, Protein: 3 g

9. Peppermint Mocha

Preparation time: 5 minutes
Cooking time: 5 minutes
Servings: 8

Ingredients:

- 4 cups 2% milk
- 1-1/2 cups brewed espresso or double-strength dark roast coffee
- Whipped cream, optional
- 8 packets of instant hot cocoa mix
- 3/4 cup peppermint schnapps liqueur

Directions:

1. Heat the milk in a big saucepan over medium heat till bubbles form around the pan's sides. Whisk in cocoa mix till blended. Put in espresso; heat through.
2. Take away from the heat; mix in liqueur. Add whipped cream (if preferred), then serve.

Nutrition: Calories: 280, Carbs: 42g, Fat: 9g, Protein: 9g

10. Mocha Frappe – Root Beer

Preparation time: 10 minutes
Cooking time: 0 minutes
Servings: 2

Ingredients:

- 1 (12 fluid oz.) can or bottle of root beer, cold
- 1 1/4 cups skim milk
- 3 tbsp sugar-free caramel flavoring syrup
- 1 tbsp imitation vanilla extract
- water, as needed
- 3 tbsp sugar-free chocolate flavoring syrup
- 2 tbsp coffee granules
- 1 tsp artificial sweetener, or to taste

Directions:

1. Add root beer into an ice cube tray, fill the tray with water as needed, and freeze for 2-3 hours until solid.
2. A blender combines sweetener, vanilla extract, coffee granules, caramel syrup, chocolate syrup, milk, and frozen root beer. Blend till smooth.

Nutrition: Calories: 218, Carbohydrate: 47.2 g, Fat: 0.1 g, Protein: 7.9 g

11. High Protein Banana Mochaccino

Preparation time: 10 minutes
Cooking time: 0 minutes
Servings: 1

Ingredients:

- 3 tbsp double-strength brewed coffee, or more to taste
- 4 bananas, frozen and chunked
- 1 tbsp chocolate-flavored protein powder
- 1 tbsp cocoa powder
- 1 cup milk
- 1 tbsp raw sunflower seed kernels
- 1 tbsp raw slivered almonds
-

Directions:

1. Fill your ice cube tray with coffee, then freeze for 6 hours overnight till completely frozen.

2. In a blender, blend cocoa, almonds, protein powder, sunflower seed kernels, banana, and two coffee ice cubes till smooth.

Nutrition: Calories: 370, Carbohydrate: 47.1 g, Fat: 14.3 g, Protein: 19 g

12. Mocha Coffee Smoothie

Preparation time: 10 minutes
Cooking time: 0 minutes
Servings: 2

Ingredients:

- 1 cup cold strong brewed coffee
- 1/3 cup white sugar
- 1/2 tsp vanilla extract
- 1 tbsp vegetable oil
- 3/4 cup powdered nondairy creamer
- 2 tbsp unsweetened cocoa powder
- 14 cubes ice
- One 5-second spray of cooking spray

Directions:

1. In a blender, place coffee and add ice, vanilla extract, cocoa, sugar, and creamer.

2. Over ice cubes, pour vegetables oil and spray into the blender with cooking spray. Blend for 1 1/2 minutes till smooth.

Nutrition: Calories: 399, Carbohydrate: 55.7 g, Fat: 20.2 g, Protein: 2.9 g

13. Choco Mocha

Preparation time: 10 minutes
Cooking time: 0 minutes
Servings: 2

Ingredients:

- 3/4 cup brewed espresso
- 1/4 cup sweetened condensed milk
- 1 cup whole milk
- 10 ice cubes, or as needed
- 3 tbsp chocolate syrup, or more to taste

Directions:

1. In a bowl, stir sweetened condensed milk and espresso together. Stir in milk and transfer to a blender.
2. Pour chocolate syrup and ice into the espresso mixture. Blend till smooth.

Nutrition: Calories: 276, Carbohydrate: 44.7 g, Fat: 7.8 g, Protein: 7.7 g

14. Hot Cocoa Mocha Coffee

Preparation time: 10 minutes
Cooking time: 0 minutes
Servings: 6 cups of mix

Ingredients:

- 2-1/2 cups powdered nondairy creamer
- 1 cup coffee granules
- 1/4 cup sugar
- 1/2 tsp ground nutmeg
- 2 cups hot cocoa mix
- 1 cup chocolate drink mix
- 2 tsp ground cinnamon
- ¾ cup boiling water

Directions:

1. Mix all the fixings in a big bowl. Keep in an airtight container.
2. Serve by adding 1 tbsp of this mix to 3/4 cup of boiling water.

Nutrition: Calories: 43, Carbohydrate: 9 g, Fat: 1 g, Protein: 0 g

15. Iced Mocha with Chocolate and Almond

Preparation time: 5 minutes
Cooking time: 0 minutes
Servings: 1

Ingredients:

- ice cubes as needed
- 1/2 cup unsweetened almond milk
- 1 1/4 cups cold coffee, divided
- 2 tbsp chocolate syrup
- 1 envelope of hot cocoa mix

Directions:

1. Add 1/4 cup of coffee to a mug, then heat for 30 seconds. Combine cocoa mix with the coffee and stir till dissolved.

2. Fill ice cubes in a big glass and pour almond milk and one cup of cold coffee over them. Mix in chocolate syrup and cocoa mixture with the almond milk and coffee.

Nutrition: Calories: 105, Carbohydrate: 16.7 g, Fat: 1.8 g, Protein: 5.2 g

16. Green Smoothie Mocha

Preparation time: 5 minutes
Cooking time: 0 minutes
Servings: 2

Ingredients:

- 2 large handfuls of green leafy veggies
- 1/2 cup almond milk
- 1 cup brewed coffee, room temperature or colder
- 1 banana
- 2 tablespoons cocoa

Directions:

1. Blend the green leafy veggies, almond milk, plus coffee in your blender until well blended.

2. Add in the remaining fixings and blend until creamy.

Nutrition: Calories: 390, Carbs: 41g, Fat: 12g, Protein: 31g

17.   Mocha Banana Milkshake

Preparation time: 5 minutes
Cooking time: 0 minutes
Servings: 3

Ingredients:

- 1 cup low-fat vanilla frozen yogurt
- 3/4 cup fat-free milk
- 1 medium ripe banana, sliced
- 1 tsp coffee granules
- 1 cup ice cubes

Directions:

1. Combine all the ingredients in a blender.
2. Cover and process the mixture for 45 to 60 seconds or until frothy.
3. Pour it into the glasses to serve.

Nutrition: Calories: 122, Carbohydrate: 24 g, Fat: 1 g, Protein: 6 g

18.   Orange Mocha

Preparation time: 5 minutes
Cooking time: 0 minutes
Servings: 1

Ingredients:

- 1 cup brewed coffee
- 2 tbsp orange juice
- 2 tbsp milk
- 1 tbsp white sugar
- 1 tbsp unsweetened cocoa powder

Directions:

1. Stir the cocoa powder, sugar, milk, orange juice, plus coffee in a mug until cocoa and sugar dissolve.
2. Serve and enjoy!

Nutrition: Calories: 92, Carbohydrate: 20.1 g, Fat: 1.5 g, Protein: 2.6 g

19.   Almond Mocha

Preparation time: 10 minutes
Cooking time: 0 minutes
Servings: 2

Ingredients:

- 1 1/2 cups warm almond milk
- 2 tbsp espresso powder
- 1/2 tsp vanilla extract
- 1 tbsp almond butter
- 1 tbsp unsweetened cocoa powder
- 1/2 tsp stevia powder

Directions:

1. Combine stevia powder, vanilla extract, cocoa powder, espresso powder, almond butter, and almond milk in a blender.
2. Mix for about 2 minutes till slightly thickened and well combined. Pour into two mugs; sprinkle with cocoa powder. Serve.

Nutrition: Calories: 115, Carbohydrate: 11.5 g, Fat: 7.1 g, Protein: 2.8 g

20.   Raspberry and Chocolate Mocha Latte

Preparation time: 5 minutes
Cooking time: 0 minutes
Servings: 1

Ingredients:

- 8 oz freshly brewed coffee
- 2 tbsp chocolate syrup
- 2 tbsp raspberry syrup
- 1/2 cup steamed milk
- Whipped cream, as you like

Directions:

1. Pour in the chocolate plus raspberry syrups into your large coffee mug.
2. Brew your coffee into your cup, then pour the steamed milk.
3. Serve it with some whipped cream plus a swirl of raspberry syrup.

Nutrition: Calories: 220, Carbs: 43g, Fat: 3g, Protein: 13g

ICED COFFEE

21. Spicy Iced Coffee

Preparation time: 10 minutes
Cooking time: 0 minutes
Servings: 2-3

Ingredients:

- 2 cups crushed ice
- 1 tsp almond extract
- 2 tbsp heavy cream
- 2 tsp grounded black cardamom
- 6 tbsp grounded coffee
- 2 tbsp sugar

Directions:

1. Blend the ground coffee and black cardamom in your blender. Use this blend to brew a pot of coffee. Add the sugar and almond to the brewed coffee, then stir well.
2. Put the brewed coffee in the fridge until fully chilled. Divide the crushed ice into 4 tall glasses.
3. Pour the chilled coffee into the glasses. Add half a spoon of cream to each glass, and serve.

Nutrition: Calories: 155, Carbs: 26g, Fat: 4g, Protein: 4g

22. Iced Café Americano Soda

Preparation time: 5 minutes
Cooking time: 0 minutes
Servings: 1

Ingredients:

- A handful of ice cubes
- 1 double shot of espresso
- 1 soda club, chilled

Directions:

1. Pour the double shot of espresso into your pint glass.
2. Fill it with ice cubes plus a soda club and stir it well. Serve immediately.

Nutrition: Calories: 10, Carbs: 2g, Fat: 10g, Protein: 0g

23. Mint-Chocolate Coffee Frappe

Preparation time: 5 minutes
Cooking time: 0 minutes
Servings: 1

Ingredients:

- 2 ounces espresso, chilled
- 1 cup ice
- Chocolate chips, to taste
- 1 cup mint chocolate chip ice cream
- 4 ounces milk
- Whipped cream, for garnish

Directions:

1. Combine the espresso, ice cream, ice, and milk in your blender, and blend until smooth.
2. Add chocolate chips, then pulse until crumbled. Top with whipped cream and.

Nutrition: Calories: 175, Carbs: 2g, Fat: 15g, Protein: 4g

24. Chai Granita

Preparation time: 5 minutes + chilling time
Cooking time: 0 minutes
Servings: 1

Ingredients:

- 3 tbsp powdered chai tea mix
- 2 tbsp of dark chocolate syrup
- 1 cup of cold coffee
- 1 can whip cream

Directions:

1. Thoroughly mix all ingredients in a shallow container. Cover the container with a lid or plastic wrap.
2. Place the container in your freezer for at least an hour. Scrape through the mixture with a fork.
3. Repeat the step every 50 minutes until the mixture is completely frozen. Top with whipped cream. Serve immediately!

Nutrition: Calories: 88, Carbs: 22g, Fat: 0g, Protein: 1g

25.   Iced Milk Coffee

Preparation time: 5 minutes
Cooking time: 0 minutes
Servings: 2-3

Ingredients:

- 2 cups crushed ice
- 2 ¼ cups of cold coffee
- 2 cups milk

Directions:

1. Slightly mix the milk and cold coffee. Pour the mixture with the crushed ice into a blender.
2. Blend until the mixture turns frothy. Serve immediately.

Nutrition: Calories: 90, Carbs: 17g, Fat: 2g, Protein: 3g

26.   Iced Coffee Slush

Preparation time: 10 minutes
Cooking time: 0 minutes
Servings: 12

Ingredients:

- 3 cups hot strong brewed coffee
- 1-1/2 to 2 cups sugar
- 4 cups milk
- 2 cups half-and-half cream
- 1-1/2 tsp vanilla extract

Directions:

1. Stir sugar and coffee in a freezer-safe bowl till sugar dissolves. Store in the fridge till thoroughly chilled. Add vanilla, cream, and milk; freeze.
2. Several hours before serving, take away from the freezer. Chop mixture till slushy, then immediately serve.

Nutrition: Calories: 202, Carbohydrate: 30 g, Fat: 7 g, Protein: 4 g

27. Cinnamon Iced Coffee Float

Preparation time: 15 minutes
Cooking time: 7-8 minutes
Servings: 1

Ingredients:

- ½ can sweeten condensed milk
- 4 cinnamon sticks
- 2 shots espresso
- Cold Cream soda, as needed
- Cinnamon sugar, as you like
- ½ cup half and half
- Dash of vanilla extract
- Ice cubes, as needed
- Vanilla ice cream, as you like

Directions:

1. In your saucepan over low heat, add the condensed milk to the half-and-half and cinnamon sticks.
2. Cook for 7-8 minutes while the cinnamon infuses. Remove from the heat, and add the vanilla extract. Remove the cinnamon sticks and pour them into a heat-proof jar.
3. Transfer the creamer to the refrigerator, where it will keep for up to 7 days.
4. Pour the espresso shot into a tall coffee glass, add the ice cubes and the churro creamer, and top up with cold cream soda.
5. Garnish with a generous scoop of ice cream and sprinkle with a little cinnamon sugar.

Nutrition: Calories: 111, Carbs: 20g, Fat: 3g, Protein: 1g

28. Strawberry Iced Coffee

Preparation time: 5 minutes
Cooking time: 0 minutes
Servings: 1

Ingredients:

- 8 ice cubes
- 1/3 cup strawberry puree
- ½ cup cold strong brewed coffee
- 1½ tbsp heavy cream

Directions:

1. Add the ice cubes to a cocktail mixer. Pour in the remaining ingredients and shake for 30-60 seconds to combine.
2. Strain into your tall glass filled with ice and serve immediately.

Nutrition: Calories: 162, Carbs: 26g, Fat: 6g, Protein: 1g

29. Almond Iced Coffee

Preparation time: 10 minutes
Cooking time: 0 minutes
Servings: 4

Ingredients:

- 12 ice cubes
- ½ tsp almond extract
- 2 cups coffee
- 1 can whip cream
- 1 tsp vanilla extract
- 3 tsp sugar
- 2 cups milk
- 2 tsp chopped almonds

Directions:

1. Mix the milk and coffee in a tall pitcher. Pour in the sugar and vanilla extract plus almond extract, and mix it well.
2. Pour the mixture into 4 glasses, and put 3 ice cubes in each glass. Add whipped cream if desired, and top it with the chopped almonds.

Nutrition: Calories: 41, Carbs: 6g, Fat: 2g, Protein: 1g

30. Toffee Iced Coffee

Preparation time: 5 minutes
Cooking time: 0 minutes
Servings: 1

Ingredients:

- 1 shot espresso
- ¼ cup toffee, chopped
- 2 scoops of vanilla ice cream

Directions:

1. Put the espresso and ice cream in a blender, and blend until smooth. Pour the mixture into a glass.
2. Top it off with the chopped toffee. Serve immediately.

Nutrition: Calories: 250, Carbs: 37g, Fat: 10g, Protein: 11g

31. Vanilla & Date Iced Coffee

Preparation time: 5 minutes
Cooking time: 0 minutes
Servings: 1-2

Ingredients:

- 1 cup chilled strong brewed coffee
- 1½ cups vanilla almond milk
- ½ cup Medjool dates, pitted & chopped
- ½ tsp vanilla
- 1 cup ice
- 1/8 tsp sea salt

Directions:

1. Add all the fixings into a blender and blitz until smooth.
2. Pour into your favorite glass and serve immediately!

Nutrition: Calories: 150, Carbs: 29g, Fat: 3g, Protein: 4g

32. Lemon Iced Coffee

Preparation time: 5 minutes
Cooking time: 0 minutes
Servings: 2

Ingredients:

- 4 tbsp sherbet lemon
- ½ tsp lemon juice
- 1 tsp grated lemon rind
- 1 tsp sugar
- ¼ cup coffee

Directions:

1. Quickly mix all the lemon ingredients in a bowl. Pour the sugar and coffee into a blender along with the lemon mixture.
2. Blend until smooth, and pour in a chilled glass with ice.
3. Serve with a slice of lemon dipped in the coffee or decorated on the side.

Nutrition: Calories: 140, Carbs: 35g, Fat: 0g, Protein: 0g

33. Creamy Decadent Iced Coffee

Preparation time: 10 minutes
Cooking time: 0 minutes
Servings: 2

Ingredients:

- 3 tbsp medium-fine ground coffee
- 2 cups ice
- 1 ½ cup filtered water

For the Cream Froth:

- ½ cup heavy cream
- ¼ tsp salt
- 1 tbsp sugar

Directions:

1. Brew the medium-fine ground coffee in your coffee maker.

2. Meanwhile, whip the heavy cream, sugar, plus salt in your bowl using a handheld milk frother until it thickens slightly within 15 seconds.

3. Slowly pour the coffee into 2 cups with ice, and pour the creamy froth on top. Serve and enjoy!

Nutrition: Calories: 228, Carbohydrates: 8g, Protein: 1g, Fat: 22g

34. Eggy Iced Coffee

Preparation time: 5 minutes
Cooking time: 0 minutes
Servings: 2

Ingredients:

- 2 cups cold milk
- 4 tbsp sugar
- 4 eggs
- 2 cups of cold coffee
- 2 tbsp nutmeg

Directions:

1. Beat the eggs plus sugar together in your bowl. Whisk in the coffee and milk, and let it chill.

2. Pour the chilled mixture into your glass. Sprinkle some nutmeg on top and serve.

Nutrition: Calories: 310, Carbs: 28g, Fat: 17g, Protein: 12g

35.   Raspberry Iced Cappuccino

Preparation time: 5 minutes
Cooking time: 0 minutes
Servings: 2

Ingredients:

- 4 ice cubes
- 1 cup of hot coffee
- 1 tbsp chocolate syrup
- 2 whole raspberries
- 1 cup milk
- 1 or ½ shot espresso
- 1 tbsp raspberry syrup

Directions:

1. Combine both syrups in the hot coffee, and stir well until the syrups dissolve.
2. Pour the milk onto the coffee, and keep it in your fridge until fully chilled.
3. Put the ice cubes in your tall glass. Pour the chilled mixture over the ice cubes. Put in the raspberries on top and serve!

Nutrition: Calories: 170, Carbs: 32g, Fat: 5g, Protein: 1g

36.   Caramel & Cinnamon Iced Coffee

Preparation time: 15 minutes
Cooking time: 0 minutes
Servings: 2

Ingredients:

- 3 ice cubes
- ½ tsp cinnamon
- ½ cup caramel syrup
- 6 tbsp ground coffee

Directions:

1. Mix the cinnamon and ground coffee, and brew a pot of coffee using this mixture.
2. Once it's done, add the caramel syrup, stir thoroughly, and let it chill in the fridge for an hour.
3. Pour the chilled coffee into your glass with ice cubes. Drizzle extra caramel syrup on top before serving.

Nutrition: Calories: 95, Carbs: 24g, Fat: 0g, Protein: 1g

37.   Honey Iced Coffee

Preparation time: 5 minutes
Cooking time: 0 minutes
Servings: 4

Ingredients:
- 1 cup ice cubes
- ¼ cup honey
- ¾ cup cold water
- 4 cups milk
- ¼ cup boiling water
- 2 tbsp coffee granules

Directions:
1. Dissolve your coffee granules in boiling water, pour the honey, and mix it well. Add cold water, and stir well until blended.
2. Pour the mixture into 4 glasses with ice, and top off 1 cup of milk for each glass. Serve and enjoy!

Nutrition: Calories: 280, Carbs: 30g, Fat: 12g, Protein: 12g

38.   Pumpkin Cold Coffee

Preparation time: 10 minutes
Cooking time: 0 minutes
Servings: 2

Ingredients:
- 1 tbsp vanilla syrup
- ¾ cup cold brew coffee
- 1 cup ice

For the Pumpkin Cream Cold Foam:
- 1/3 cup half & half
- 1 tbsp pumpkin sauce
- 1 tbsp vanilla syrup
- ¼ tsp pumpkin spice

Directions:
1. Pour half & half vanilla syrup plus pumpkin sauce into your French press.
2. Put the lid, then move the plunger up and down 40 times. Set aside.
3. Put the vanilla syrup, cold brew, plus ice into your cup, and top it with the cold foam plus dust of pumpkin spice. Serve and enjoy!

Nutrition: Calories: 360, Carbs: 48g, Fat: 17g, Protein: 4g

39. White Mocha Granita

Preparation time: 5 minutes
Cooking time: 0 minutes
Servings: 1

Ingredients:

- 3 tbsp white chocolate syrup
- ½ cup milk
- 1 cup of cold coffee

Directions:

1. Pour the coffee plus milk into your bowl, and mix in the chocolate syrup. Keep in your fridge, and let it chill within 1 hour.
2. Scrape the mixture every 45 minutes using a fork until fully frozen.
3. Scrape the frozen mixture 1 more time before serving. Enjoy!

Nutrition: Calories: 324, Carbs: 25g, Fat: 12g, Protein: 6g

40. Coconut Ice Coffee

Preparation time: 5 minutes
Cooking time: 0 minutes
Servings: 1

Ingredients:

- 1 cup of any brand of coconut water
- ½ cup cold brew coffee
- Coconut flavored creamer

Directions:

1. Combine the coconut water plus cold brew in your tall glass and top with ice.
2. Pour a little coconut creamer over the top but don't stir. Serve immediately!

Nutrition: Calories: 106, Carbs: 11g, Fat: 11g, Protein: 1g

41. High Protein Chocolate Iced Coffee

Preparation time: 5 minutes
Cooking time: 0 minutes
Servings: 2

Ingredients:

- ½ cup whole milk
- 1 cup strong brewed coffee (room temperature)
- 2 tsp sweetened cocoa powder
- 6 drops stevia
- 1 scoop chocolate-flavored protein
- ½ tsp sea salt

Directions:

1. Add all fixings into a blender and blend until smooth.
2. Pour into two glasses and top with plenty of ice. Serve immediately!

Nutrition: Calories: 98, Carbs: 2g, Fat: 2g, Protein: 18g

42. Iced Coffee Colada

Preparation time: 5 minutes
Cooking time: 0 minutes
Servings: 2

Ingredients:

- 2 ounces espresso
- 1 cup 1% milk
- 5 ounces piña colada coffee syrup
- 1 scoop of vanilla protein powder

Directions:

1. Brew the coffee in your preferred way. Pour the coffee over ice to cool it down quickly. Add the milk and piña colada syrup.
2. Transfer the mixture to your blender and blitz until silky. Serve and ejoy!

Nutrition: Calories: 100, Carbs: 16g, Fat: 3g, Protein: 4g

43. Fruit Iced Coffee

Preparation time: 5 minutes
Cooking time: 0 minutes
Servings: 1-2

Ingredients:

- ½ cup of ice cubes
- 2 Brazilian nuts, chopped
- ½ tsp shredded coconut
- 2 tbsp peanut butter
- 3 tsp brown sugar
- 1 shot of cold espresso
- 1/2 cup vanilla frozen yogurt
- 1 banana
- 4 ½ strips dried mango, chopped
- ¼ cup coconut cream
- 1 tsp unsalted roasted peanuts, grind
- ½ tsp cereal or rice crispies
- 1 shot of hot espresso

Directions:

1. Stir the brown sugar into the hot espresso, and let it cool.

2. Combine the hot espresso, cold espresso, banana, coconut cream, grounded peanuts, peanut butter, yogurt, ice, plus brown sugar in a blender, and blend until smooth.

3. Pour the mixture into a chilled glass, and stir in the mango and Brazilian nuts. Top it off with the shredded coconut and cereal or rice crispies. Serve and enjoy!

Nutrition: Calories: 100, Carbs: 16g, Fat: 3g, Protein: 4g

44. Ice Cream Coke Coffee Float

Preparation time: 5 minutes
Cooking time: 0 minutes
Servings: 4

Ingredients:

- 1 can Coca-Cola
- 2 ½ cups of coffee
- 1 cup light cream
- 4 scoops of coffee-flavored ice cream

Directions:

1. Mix the light cream and the coffee, and pour the mixture into 4 glasses, each one-half full.

2. Top each glass with the ice cream, and divide the can of Coca-Cola in each glass. Serve and enjoy!

Nutrition: Calories: 280, Carbs: 48g, Fat: 9g, Protein: 4g

CAPPUCCINO

45.   Chocolate & Cherry Cappuccino

Preparation time: 10 minutes
Cooking time: 0 minutes
Servings: 6 cups of mix

Ingredients:

- 3 cups sugar
- 1-1/3 cups powdered non-dairy creamer
- 1 cup baking cocoa
- 2 cups confectioners' sugar
- 1-1/3 cups coffee granules
- 1 envelope (.13 oz.) unsweetened cherry mix

For serving:

- 1 cup hot 2% milk
- 2 tbsp miniature marshmallows

Directions:

1. Combine the confectioners' sugar, regular sugar, powdered non-dairy creamer, coffee granules, baking cocoa, plus unsweetened cherry mix in your big airtight container.
2. Keep for up to 2 months in a cool and dry place until ready to serve.

For cappuccino:

3. Place 2 tbsp prepared cherry choco-cappuccino mix in your mug, then add in hot milk and stir till combined. Add marshmallow on top before serving.

Nutrition: Calories: 259, Carbohydrate: 37 g, Fat: 9 g, Protein: 9 g

46. Cold Caramel Cappuccino

Preparation time: 10 minutes
Cooking time: 0 minutes
Servings: 2

Ingredients:

- 1 cup half-and-half cream
- 3 tbsp + 2 tsp caramel ice cream topping, divided
- 8 to 10 ice cubes
- 1 cup 2% milk
- 2 tsp coffee granules
- 4 tbsp whipped cream

Directions:

1. Mix the ice cubes, coffee granules, 3 tbsp caramel topping, milk plus half-and-half in your blender and blend until smooth.
2. Transfer to your 2 chilled glasses, place the whipped cream on top, and drizzle with the leftover caramel topping. Serve and enjoy!

Nutrition: Calories: 337, Carbohydrate: 36 g, Fat: 16 g, Protein: 9 g

47. Cappuccino Cooler

Preparation time: 5 minutes
Cooking time: 0 minutes
Servings: 4

Ingredients:

- 1 1/2 cups cold coffee
- 1 1/2 cups chocolate ice cream
- 1/4 cup chocolate syrup
- crushed ice, as needed
- 1 cup whipped cream

Directions:

1. Combine chocolate syrup, ice cream, and coffee in a blender, then blend till smooth.
2. Over crushed ice, pour the mixture and use a dollop of whipped cream for garnish. Serve.

Nutrition: Calories: 199, Carbohydrate: 28 g, Fat: 9 g, Protein: 2.9 g

48.   Matcha Latte Cappuccino

Preparation time: 5 minutes
Cooking time: 0 minutes
Servings: 1

Ingredients:

- 2 tsp granulated sugar
- ¼ cup of water at room temperature
- ½ cup milk
- 2 tsp high-quality matcha
- 6 ice cubes crushed
- 2 oz brewed hot espresso

Directions:

1. Put the sugar plus matcha in your tall glass, add water and mix it well until blended. Add the crushed ice cubes to your glass.

2. Position the back of your spoon slightly above the ice, and slowly pour the milk over the back of your spoon.

3. Lastly, gently pour the hot espresso over the back of your spoon on top of the milk plus ice. Stir and enjoy!

Nutrition: Calories: 79, Carbohydrates: 10g, Protein: 5g, Fat: 2g

49.   French Vanilla Cappuccino

Preparation time: 5 minutes
Cooking time: 0 minutes
Servings: 4 cups mix

Ingredients:

- 3 cup sugar
- 2 cups instant hot cocoa mix
- 2 cup confectioners' sugar
- 2 jar (16 oz.) French Vanilla powdered non-dairy creamer
- 2 cup nonfat dry milk powder
- 1 cup coffee granules

For serving:

- 1 cup hot water
- Sweetened whipped cream and baking cocoa, as you like

Directions:

1. Mix all the fixings in your bowl except for the serving fixings. Put in your airtight container for up to 2 months in a cool and dry place.

For cappuccino:

2. Put in 1/4 cup of French vanilla cappuccino mix in your coffee mug and add 1 cup of hot water.

3. Stir until well combined, then place whipped cream on top and drizzle with baking cocoa.

Nutrition: Calories: 186, Carbohydrate: 32 g, Fat: 4 g, Protein: 3 g

50. Salted Caramel & Choco Frappuccino

Preparation time: 5 minutes
Cooking time: 0 minutes
Servings: 1

Ingredients:
- 2 cups ice
- ½ cup half & half
- 3 tbsp salted caramel syrup
- ¼ cup coffee
- 1-2 tbsp chocolate sauce
-

Directions:

1. Put all the fixings in a blender, and blend until well combined.

2. Add the remaining chocolate syrup, then pour into a glass; top with whipped cream and chocolate syrup if preferred.

Nutrition: Calories: 330, Carbs: 53g, Fat: 12g, Protein: 4g

51. Cappuccino Punch

Preparation time: 10 minutes
Cooking time: 0 minutes
Servings: about 19 cups

Ingredients:
- 1/2 cup sugar
- 1 cup boiling water
- 1-quart vanilla ice cream softened
- Grated chocolate, optional
- 1/4 cup coffee granules
- 2 quarts of whole milk
- 1-quart chocolate ice cream softened

Directions:

1. Mix the coffee and sugar; add boiling water and stir until dissolved. Cover and store in the fridge until chilled.

2. Transfer the mixture into your big punch bowl right before serving. Mix in the milk, and stir in scoops of ice cream until melted. Drizzle with grated chocolate if preferred.

Nutrition: Calories: 238, Carbohydrate: 29 g, Fat: 11 g, Protein: 7 g

52. White Chocolate Cappuccino

Preparation time: 5 minutes
Cooking time: 5 minutes
Servings: 1

Ingredients:
- 2 tbsp white chocolate chips
- 1 tbsp white chocolate-flavored syrup
- ½ cup milk
- ½ cup hot freshly brewed coffee

Directions:
1. Place white chocolate chips in your mug.
2. Heat the milk and white chocolate syrup in your saucepan over medium heat. Froth the hot milk using your immersion blender.
3. Pour hot coffee over chocolate chips. Carefully pour frothed milk over your brewed coffee. Serve and enjoy!

Nutrition: Calories: 78, Carbs: 0g, Fat: 0g, Protein: 2g

53. Honey Cappuccino

Preparation time: 5 minutes
Cooking time: 0 minutes
Servings: 2

Ingredients:
- 2 tsp honey, + more for topping
- 2 shots of espresso or more
- ½ cup steamed almond milk & foam

Directions:
1. Add the honey to your mug.
2. Pour some steamed milk and stir until well blended with the honey.
3. Add the espresso shots, then pour the rest of your steamed milk plus the foam. Drizzle honey over the top. Serve and enjoy!

Nutrition: Calories: 280, Carbs: 52g, Fat: 5g, Protein: 6g

54. Cappuccino Smoothies

Preparation time: 5 minutes
Cooking time: 0 minutes
Servings: 3

Ingredients:

- 1 cup (8 oz.) cappuccino
- 1/3 cup whole milk
- 3 tbsp confectioners' sugar, optional
- 1 tbsp chocolate syrup
- 1-1/2 cups ice cubes
- 1/2 cup miniature marshmallows, divided

Directions:

1. Combine chocolate syrup, sugar (if preferred), milk, and yogurt in a blender—place in 1/4 cup of marshmallows and ice cubes.
2. Cover then process until blended, and transfer into chilled glasses. Place the leftover marshmallows on top, then immediately serve.

Nutrition: Calories: 166, Carbohydrate: 30 g, Fat: 3 g, Protein: 5 g

55. Caramel Mochaccino

Preparation time: 5 minutes
Cooking time: 0 minutes
Servings: 2

Ingredients:

- 4 tbsp brewed coffee
- 3 cups ice
- 1/4 cup caramel sauce
- 1/4 cup milk of choice

Directions:

1. Place all ingredients in a blender. Blend until well combined.
2. Pour into two pretty glasses. Top with some more caramel sauce and servee.

Nutrition: Calories: 140, Carbs: 25g, Fat: 3g, Protein: 3g

56.   Double-Chocolate Cappuccino

Preparation time: 5 minutes
Cooking time: 5 minutes
Servings: 8

Ingredients:

- 1 cup whipping (heavy) cream
- 1 tsp + 2 tbsp dry espresso coffee, divided
- ½ cup baking cocoa
- 8 cinnamon sticks
- 1 tbsp + 1/3 cup packed brown sugar, divided
- 8 cups milk
- 4 oz sweet baking chocolate, cut up

Directions:

1. In your small chilled bowl, beat whipping cream, 1 tbsp brown sugar, plus 1 tsp espresso coffee using your electric mixer on almost max speed.

2. Cover and refrigerate until you are not going to serve.

3. shuffle cocoa, milk, 1/3 cup brown sugar plus 2 tbsp espresso coffee in your 3-quart saucepan. Heat over medium heat, just to simmer, often stirring.

4. Stir in chocolate until it is completely melted. Pour the mixture into cups. Top each cup with the whipped cream. Add the cinnamon sticks and serve!

57.   Turtle Cappuccino

Preparation time: 5 minutes
Cooking time: 0 minutes
Servings: 1

Ingredients:

- 3/4 oz. caramel sauce
- 1/2 oz. macadamia nut syrup
- 1 cup steamed milk
- 3/4 oz. dark chocolate sauce
- 3 oz. espresso

Directions:

1. Combine all the fixings except steamed milk in your cup, stir well until blended and set aside.

2. Pour the steamed milk on top and gently stir. Garnish on top, if desired, then serve and enjoy!

Preparation time: 5 minutes
Cooking time: 0 minutes
Servings: 4

Ingredients:

- 1 cup milk
- 1 cup strong cold-brewed coffee
- 1/2 cup whipped topping, thawed frozen
- 2 (3.1 oz.) milk chocolate bar
- 2 cup coffee ice cream
- 2 tbsp chocolate syrup, divided
- 4 Honey Grahams, each broken into 4 rectangles, divided
- 4 marshmallows, already toasted, each threaded onto a little stick
- 4 tsp marshmallow creme

Directions:

1. Break each chocolate bar into 12 pieces; set aside 2 pieces for later use.
2. Crush your 1 small graham rectangle and place it in your shallow dish. Reserve remaining graham rectangles.
3. Spread the marshmallow creme onto the rims the glasses. Dip the rims, one at a time, into your graham crumbs, turning until evenly coated.
4. Pour 2 tsp chocolate syrup inside each glass; for later use.
5. Blend the milk, ice cream, coffee, the remaining graham rectangles, plus any remaining graham crumbs in your blender. Pour the ice cream mixture into your glasses.
6. Add two tbsp whipped topping, the pierced marshmallows, 1 of the chocolate rectangles you put aside, and remaining graham
7. Cover with the chocolate syrup.

Nutrition: Calories: 140, Carbs: 23g, Fat: 5g, Protein: 1g

59. Choco & Peanut Butter Frappuccino

Preparation time: 5 minutes
Cooking time: 0 minutes
Servings: 1-2

Ingredients:

- ¾ cup strong brewed coffee (cold)
- 1 tbsp. Dutch-processed cocoa powder
- 2 cups ice
- ½ tsp smooth peanut butter
- ½ cup skimmed milk
- 1 tbsp. peanut butter powder
- Few drops stevia

Directions:

1. Add all the fixings into a blender and blitz until smooth. Pour into your favorite glass.

2. Warm the smooth peanut butter in the microwave and then drizzle over the Frappuccino. Serve immediately!

Nutrition: Calories: 251, Carbs: 37g, Fat: 1g, Protein: 26g

60. Frappuccino & Biscotti

Preparation time: 5 minutes
Cooking time: 0 minutes
Servings: 2

Ingredients:

- 2 pieces of biscotti + crumbs
- 1 ½ cups milk
- 1 ½ cups vanilla ice cream
- 1 ½ cup fresh coffee
- a dash of Amaretto (optional)

Directions:

1. Add the coffee and milk into a blender, and blend until well combined.

2. Add the vanilla ice cream, biscotti, and 1 cup of ice. Blend until smooth.

3. Serve in 2 tall glasses, and sprinkle biscotti crumbs on top to garnish. If you don't have crumbs, pulse another biscotti in the blender to create some.

Nutrition: Calories: 110, Carbs: 17g, Fat: 4g, Protein: 3g

WHITE COFFEE

61. Cinnamon White Latte

Preparation time: 5 minutes
Cooking time: 5 minutes
Servings: 4

Ingredients:

- 2 tbsp cream cheese, softened
- 4 tbsp erythritol sweetener
- 4 tsp cinnamon
- 8 oz almond milk, unsweetened
- 2 tsp vanilla extract, unsweetened
- 4 tbsp whipping cream
- 3/2 cup brewed white coffee

Directions:

1. Take a medium pot, place it over medium heat, add milk
2. Mix cinnamon, vanilla, sweetener, and cream cheese.
3. Cook for 4 minutes and wait until the cream has dissolved, keeping stirring.
4. Divide coffee between 4 cups, pour in cream cheese mixture and then top each cup with a tbsp of cream.

Nutrition: Calories: 274, Carbs: 47g, Fat: 4g, Protein: 12g

62. Banana White Coffee

Preparation time: 5 minutes
Cooking time: 0 minutes
Servings: 2

Ingredients:

- 1 cup milk
- ice cubes
- 1 very ripe banana
- 1 cup cold brewed white coffee

Directions:

1. Blend the banana and milk for 1 minute in a blender until smooth.
2. Fill ice cubes into two 16-oz. glasses. Pour the white coffee among the glasses and top with banana milk, then divide it between the glasses evenly.

Nutrition: Calories: 133, Carbohydrate: 23.9 g, Fat: 2.6 g, Protein: 4.8 g

63.   Homemade Iced Salted Caramel White Espresso

Preparation time: 5 minutes
Cooking time: 0 minutes
Servings: 1

Ingredients:

- 2 oz white espresso, chilled
- 1 cup ice
- 2 tbsp caramel sauce
- Whipped cream, for garnish
- 1 cup vanilla ice cream
- 4 oz milk
- ½ tsp salt

Directions:

1. Combine the white espresso, ice cream, ice, milk, caramel sauce, plus salt in your blender, and blend until smooth.
2. Transfer to your glass, then top it with whipped cream, as desired, plus a drizzle of caramel sauce.

Nutrition: Calories: 150, Carbs: 22g, Fat: 5g, Protein: 6g\

64.   Maple White Coffee

Preparation time: 7 minutes
Cooking time: 5-6 minutes
Servings: 2

Ingredients:

- 4 oz white espresso
- 20 oz milk
- 2 to 4 tablespoons pure maple syrup
- some ground cinnamon, for topping

Directions:

1. Pour the white espresso into a mug and stir in the maple syrup.
2. Heat the milk in your saucepan over medium heat for 5 minutes until about to boil (but not boil it).
3. Froth the milk until it thickens within 20 to 30 seconds with a milk frother.
4. Swirl the glass and tap it gently on the table so that the bubbles disappear.
5. Pour the milk into the espresso while retaining the foam with a spoon. Now add the remaining foam to the top. Sprinkle the latte with cinnamon.

Nutrition: Calories: 212, Carbs: 32g, Fat: 5g, Protein: 10g

65. Lemon White Coffee

Preparation time: 10 minutes
Cooking time: 0 minutes
Servings: 3

Ingredients:

- 2 cups brewed white coffee, chilled
- 1 cup lemon sherbet, softened
- 2 tbsp sugar
- 1 tbsp lemon juice
- Lemon peel, optional

Directions:

1. Add lemon juice, sugar, sherbet, and white coffee to a blender. Cover and process till smooth.
2. Transfer into chilled glasses. Add lemon peel to garnish if preferred. Immediately serve.

Nutrition: Calories: 105, Carbohydrate: 24 g, Fat: 1 g, Protein: 1 g

66. Homemade Superfood White Coffee

Preparation time: 5 minutes
Cooking time: 0 minutes
Servings: 1

Ingredients:

- 1 cup of white coffee
- 1 tbsp cacao nibs
- 1 tsp coconut oil
- ½ tsp turmeric
- Pinch of cayenne pepper
- 1 cup almond milk
- 1 tsp maca powder
- 1 tsp honey
- ½ tsp vanilla extract
- Cinnamon to sprinkle

Directions:

1. Blend the cacao nibs, almond milk, plus white coffee in your blender until well blended.
2. Add the remaining fixings, then serve and enjoy!

Nutrition: Calories: 190, Carbs: 44g, Fat: 1g, Protein: 2g

67. Molten Chocolate Iced White Latte

Preparation time: 5 minutes
Cooking time: 0 minutes
Servings: 2

Ingredients:

- 2 cups brewed white coffee, cold
- 2 tbsp cream cheese, softened
- 1/4 cup heavy whipping cream
- 2 tbsp white chocolate sauce
- 1 tbsp sugar
- 4 ice cubes, or as desired

Directions:

1. Combine the ice cubes, cream, sugar, cream cheese, white chocolate sauce, and white coffee in your blender.
2. Blend until cream cheese is smooth. Serve in your glasses, and enjoy!

Nutrition: Calories: 216, Carbohydrate: 15.4 g, Fat: 16.3 g, Protein: 2.4 g

68. Cappuccino Blanco

Preparation time: 10 minutes
Cooking time: 5 minutes
Servings: 2

Ingredients:

- ½ cup milk, 2% milkfat
- 1 vanilla bean, split
- 1 tsp light brown sugar
- 6 oz freshly brewed white espresso
- ground cinnamon, as you like

Directions:

1. In your small saucepan, combine the milk plus vanilla. Scald the milk, and remove from heat. Cover and let the milk steep within 5 minutes.
2. Stir the sugar into the milk, reheat slightly and remove the vanilla bean.
3. Transfer the milk to your blender, and blend until frothy, within 45 seconds. Pour the hot white espresso into your 2 warmed, 8-ounce coffee mugs.
4. Add the hot milk, and sprinkle with cinnamon before serving.

Nutrition: Calories: 51, Carbs: 2g, Fat: 1g, Protein: 1g

69. White Coffee with Gingerbread

Preparation time: 10 minutes
Cooking time: 0 minutes
Servings: 6

Ingredients:

- 1/2 cup molasses
- 1/2 tsp baking soda
- 3/4 tsp ground cinnamon
- 1 cup half-and-half cream
- 1 1/2 cups sweetened whipped cream
- 1/4 cup brown sugar
- 1 tsp ground ginger
- 6 cups hot brewed white coffee
- 1 tsp ground cloves

Directions:

1. Combine the cinnamon, ginger, baking soda, brown sugar, and molasses in a small bowl to blend well. Cover and place in your fridge within 10 minutes.
2. To each cup, add about 1/4 cup of white coffee. Mix in about a tbsp of spice mixture till it dissolves.
3. Within an inch of the top, fill in coffee then mix in half-and-half to taste. Add a light sprinkle of cloves and whipped cream to garnish.

Nutrition: Calories: 198, Carbohydrate: 30.6 g, Fat: 8.1 g, Protein: 2 g

70. Flat White Espresso

Preparation time: 5 minutes
Cooking time: 0 minutes
Servings: 2

Ingredients:

- 2 shots of white espresso
- 1 cup milk steamed
- sugar to taste (optional)

Directions:

1. Prepare your espresso shots and pour them into your glass over the sugar (if using).
2. Steam your milk, then froth the milk within 1 minute using a frother. Pour the hot frothy foamed milk over your espresso and serve!

Nutrition: Calories: 156, Carbohydrates: 13g, Protein: 7g, Fat: 8g

71.   Tropical Spiced White Coffee

Preparation time: 10 minutes
Cooking time: 5 minutes
Servings: 9

Ingredients:

- 3/4 cup ground white coffee
- 1 cup water
- 3 cinnamon sticks (3 inches)
- 2 tbsp unsweetened pineapple juice
- 1 tsp grated lemon peel
- 3/4 cup packed brown sugar
- 2 fresh orange slices
- 1/2 tsp vanilla extract

Directions:

1. Add the coffee grounds to a coffeemaker's basket or filter—place in lemon peel. Follow the manufacturer's directions to prepare 9 cups of brewed coffee.
2. Combine the vanilla, pineapple juice, orange slices, cinnamon sticks, brown sugar, and water in a small saucepan.
3. Cook while stirring till the sugar dissolved over medium heat. Strain; remove oranges and cinnamon—transfer sugar mixture into mugs. Pour in coffee and stir.

Nutrition: Calories: 90, Carbohydrate: 22 g, Fat: 0 g, Protein: 1 g

72.   White Coffee Ice Cream Float

Preparation time: 15 minutes
Cooking time: 0 minutes
Servings: 1

Ingredients:

- 1 shot of white espresso, cold
- 3 scoops of vanilla ice cream
- 1 chocolate chip cookie or brownie, small
- 6 & 3/4 fl. oz. whole milk
- 2 cubes of ice
-

Directions:

1. Pour the white espresso and milk into your blender. Add two scoops of ice cream plus cubed ice, and blend until smooth.
2. Pour the drink into your tall glass, top it with the remaining ice cream plus crumble the top with a cookie or brownie to garnish. Serve.

Nutrition: Calories: 310, Carbs: 28g, Fat: 20g, Protein: 5g

73. Cardamom White Coffee

Preparation time: 5 minutes
Cooking time: 0 minutes
Servings: 2

Ingredients:

- 1 tablespoon maple syrup
- ½ cup milk
- 2 cups brewed white coffee
- 4 cardamom pods
- Ice, as needed

Directions:

1. Place the cardamom pods and maple syrup in the hot white coffee and stir.
2. Let it cool.
3. Add the milk and pour into a glass with ice.

Nutrition: Calories: 573, Carbs: 54g, Fat: 37g, Protein: 6g

74. Strawberry Iced White Coffee

Preparation time: 5 minutes
Cooking time: 0 minutes
Servings: 1

Ingredients:

- 1 cup milk
- 1 tbsp water
- Whipped cream
- 1 tbsp white coffee granules
- 2 tbsp strawberry ice cream for topping
- sugar to taste

Directions:

1. Combine all the fixings in your blender until well blended.
2. Decorate with whipped cream. Serve and enjoy!

Nutrition: Calories: 164, Carbs: 40g, Fat: 1g, Protein: 2g

75. White Coffee with Cinnamon & Cloves

Preparation time: 5 minutes
Cooking time: 0 minutes
Servings: 2

Ingredients:

- 2 cups water
- 1/2 cinnamon stick (3 inches)
- 5 tsp sugar
- 5 tsp white coffee granules
- 4 whole cloves
- whipped topping, optional

Directions:

1. Combine the cloves, cinnamon stick, white coffee granules, and water in your small saucepan, and let it boil. Remove and let it stand with the cover for 5-8 minutes.
2. Strain and remove spices, add in sugar and stir until dissolved. Pour into mugs, add whipped topping (if preferred), then serve.

Nutrition: Calories: 46, Carbohydrate: 11 g, Fat: 0 g, Protein: 0 g

76. Cookie Iced White Coffee

Preparation time: 5 minutes
Cooking time: 0 minutes
Servings: 3

Ingredients:

- 18 oz. brewed white coffee
- 1 tbsp vanilla
- 9 oz. milk
- 2,5 cookie dough ice cream scoops
- 1/3 cup mini chocolate cookies
- 1 tbsp brown sugar

Directions:

1. Pour the milk, coffee, and vanilla into the blender and add the ice cream, cookies, and sugar. Blend until you get a homogeneous mixture.
2. Pour into a glass with ice and serve.

Nutrition: Calories: 200, Carbs: 37g, Fat: 6g, Protein: 2g

77. Hazelnut Iced White Coffee

Preparation time: 5 minutes
Cooking time: 0 minutes
Servings: 2

Ingredients:

- 2 tbsp white ground coffee
- 2 tbsp milk
- 1 tsp hazelnut syrup
- A pinch of chocolate powder
- 1 cup ice

Directions:

1. Brew 2 rounded tbsp of ground white coffee in your drip coffee maker.
2. In your tall glass, pour in milk, hazelnut syrup, plus a pinch of hot chocolate powder, and mix it well.
3. Add the ice and slowly pour your brewed white coffee. Stir and serve!

Nutrition: Calories: 180, Carbs: 29g, Fat: 7g, Protein: 1g

78. White Coffee Cappuccino with Coconut

Preparation time: 5 minutes
Cooking time: 5 minutes
Servings: 1

Ingredients:

- 2 shots of white espresso
- 1/3 cup coconut milk
- A pinch cinnamon

Directions:

1. Heat 1/3 cup coconut milk in your saucepan and froth.
2. Pour the frothy coconut milk using your large spoon to hold back the foam over the white espresso shots until the cup is 2/3 full.
3. Spoon the foam on top and add a pinch of cinnamon. Serve and enjoy!

Nutrition: Calories: 81, Carbs: 14g, Fat: 2g, Protein: 1g

DALGONA

79.   Chai Dalgona Latte

Preparation time: 5 minutes
Servings: 1

Ingredients:

- 1 handful ice
- 1 tsp sugar
- 1 tsp chai tea powder

- 1 tsp coffee granules
- 1 tbsp hot water
- 1 cup of milk of your choice

Directions:

1. Add the coffee, sugar, plus hot water to your bowl and whisk until stiff peaks.
2. Combine the chai tea powder plus milk in your glass and mix it well.
3. Add ice and spoon the whipped coffee mixture on top. Serve and enjoy!

Nutrition: Calories: 60, Carbs: 10g, Fat: 2g, Protein: 1g

80.   Vanilla & Cinnamon Dalgona Coffee

Preparation time: 5 minutes
Cooking time: 0 minutes
Servings: 1

Ingredients:

- 2 tbsp boiling water
- 2 tsp coffee granules
- 1 cup milk
- Ice, as needed

- 1 tbsp granulated sugar
- 1/8 tsp ground cinnamon
- 1/8 tsp vanilla extract
-

Directions:

1. Place the boiling water, sugar, ground coffee, plus cinnamon in your medium bowl, and mix until well combined. Beat using your electric mixer until stiff peaks form within 2 minutes.
2. Mix the milk plus vanilla in your glass, and add ice as needed.
3. Spoon the whipped coffee mixture over your vanilla milk. Sprinkle with additional cinnamon, if you like. Serve and enjoy!

Nutrition: Calories: 220, Carbs: 34g, Fat: 7g, Protein: 5g

81. Caramel Dalgona Coffee

Preparation time: 5 minutes
Cooking time: 0 minutes
Servings: 1

Ingredients:

- 1 tbsp coffee granules
- 1 tbsp sugar
- 1 tbsp hot water
- 2 ice cubes
- 1 cup cold milk
- 2 tbsp caramel syrup, + more or less as needed

Directions:

1. Combine the coffee granules, sugar, and hot water in your small bowl. Whip using your electric mixer until fluffy.
2. Put the ice cubes in your glass and pour the milk. Add your caramel syrup and stir well. Spoon the whipped coffee on top, serve and enjoy!

Nutrition: Calories: 60, Carbs: 14g, Fat: 0g, Protein: 1g

82. Coconut Sugar Dalgona

Preparation time: 5 minutes
Cooking time: 0 minutes
Servings: 1

Ingredients:

- 2 tbsp coffee granules
- 2 tbsp coconut sugar
- 2 tbsp hot water
- 1 cup warm or iced milk

Directions:

1. Mix the coffee granules, coconut sugar, plus hot water into your bowl. Whip the coffee using your electric mixer until it thickens
2. Dollop the whipped coffee on top of your milk and serve!

Nutrition: Calories: 190, Carbs: 30g, Fat: 7g, Protein: 1g

83. Pumpkin Dalgona Coffee

Preparation time: 5 minutes
Cooking time: 0 minutes
Servings: 2

Ingredients:

- 2 tbsp coffee granules
- 2 tbsp boiling water
- 1/2 tsp pumpkin spice
- 2 cups milk

- 2 tbsp granulated sugar
- 1 tsp vanilla extract
- 2 cups ice
-

Directions:

1. Combine the coffee granules, sugar, boiling water, pumpkin spice, and vanilla extract in your medium bowl. Whip using your hand mixer until soft peaks, within 2 minutes.
2. Put 1 cup ice plus 1 cup milk in your 2 coffee mugs, and divide the whipped coffee between your two mugs. Serve and enjoy!

Nutrition: Calories: 140, Carbs: 24g, Fat: 5g, Protein: 1g

84. Nutella Dalgona Coffee

Preparation time: 5 minutes
Cooking time: 0 minutes
Servings: 1

Ingredients:

- 1 tbsp ground coffee
- 2 tbsp hot water
- 1 cup milk

- 2 tbsp granulated sugar
- 1 tbsp Nutella
- ice cubes (optional)

Directions:

1. Add the ground coffee, sugar, plus hot water to your bowl, and whip using your electric mixer on medium-high speed until thick within 5-6 minutes.
2. Gently mix the Nutella into your coffee mixture using your spatula, but do not overmix.
3. Pour the milk, then add the ice cubes into your cup. Spoon the whipped coffee Nutella mixture on top, and serve!

Nutrition: Calories: 169, Carbs: 38g, Fat: 1g, Protein: 3g

85. Hazelnut Dalgona Coffee

Preparation time: 5 minutes
Cooking time: 0 minutes
Servings: 1

Ingredients:

- 2 tbsp hazelnut flavored syrup
- 2 tbsp hot water
- 2 tbsp coffee granules
- 1 cup chilled almond milk

Directions:

1. Whip the coffee granules, hazelnut syrup, plus hot water within a few minutes until it thickens.

2. Pour the almond milk into your glass, then spoon the whipped hazelnut coffee mixture on top. Serve and enjoy!

Nutrition: Calories: 35, Carbs: 5g, Fat: 2g, Protein: 0g

86. Samoa Dalgona Coffee

Preparation time: 5 minutes
Cooking time: 0 minutes
Servings: 1-2

Ingredients:

- 2 tbsp toasted coconut shreds
- 6 oz milk
- ½ tsp coconut syrup
- ¼ cup boiling water
- 1 tbsp shredded coconut
- 2 tbsp caramel sauce
- 3 ice cubes
- ¼ cup espresso powder
- ¼ cup brown sugar
- Drizzle of chocolate syrup

Directions:

1. Rim your glass with caramel sauce, then dip the rim in your toasted coconut. Pour the milk into your favorite glass.

2. Add the coconut syrup plus ice cubes to your glass. Keep it in your freezer for a while.

3. Place the espresso powder, boiling water, plus sugar in your bowl and whip using your electric mixer until peaks form.

4. Top the chilled milk mixture with the whipped coffee. Drizzle with more caramel sauce, chocolate syrup, plus toasted coconut shreds as you like. Serve and enjoy!

Nutrition: Calories: 167, Carbs: 23g, Fat: 8g, Protein: 2g

87. Matcha Dalgona Coffee

Preparation time: 5 minutes
Servings: 1

Ingredients:

- 1 cup ice
- 2 tbsp hot water
- 1 tbsp sugar

- 1/3 cup milk
- 1 tbsp coffee granules

For the Sweetened Matcha:

- 2 tbsp water
- 1/2 tsp matcha

- 1 tbsp sugar

Directions:

1. Combine the coffee granules, sugar, plus hot water in your bowl and whip using your electric mixer until soft peaks form.

2. Whip the matcha, sugar, plus water in a separate bowl until no matcha clumps are found. Pour the sweetened matcha into your cup, and add the ice.

3. Slowly add the milk to your ice, and spoon the whipped coffee mixture on top. Serve and enjoy!

Nutrition: Calories: 200, Carbs: 26g, Fat: 8g, Protein: 5g

88. Orange Choco Dalgona Coffee

Preparation time: 5 minutes
Servings: 2-3

Ingredients:

- 6 tbsp coffee granules
- 6 tbsp hot water
- 2 tsp cocoa powder
- 2 cups milk
- 2 pinches of grated nutmeg

- 6 tbsp granulated sugar
- 2 tsp orange juice
- Ice cubes, as needed
- 2 pinches of orange zest
-

Directions:

1. Combine the coffee granules, granulated sugar, hot water, orange juice, plus cocoa powder in your mixing bowl.

2. Beat them within 3-5 minutes using your hand-held electric mixer on high speed until it forms a stiff peak.

3. Fill your two mugs halfway with ice, then pour the milk over. Top it with the whipped coffee mixture and garnish with the orange zest plus nutmeg. Serve and enjoy!

Nutrition: Calories: 160, Carbs: 19g, Fat: 8g, Protein: 2g

89. Oreo Dalgona Coffee

Preparation time: 5 minutes
Servings: 1

Ingredients:
- 2 tbsp coffee granules
- 2 tbsp boiling water
- Ice, as needed (optional)
- 2 tbsp granulated sugar
- 1 cup milk
- Oreos, as you like

Directions:

1. Mix the coffee, sugar, and boiling water into your small bowl, and whip within 2 minutes until it becomes creamy foam.

2. Add crushed Oreos, ice, plus almond milk to your glass. Spoon the whipped coffee mixture on top. Add more crushed Oreos on top, and serve.

Nutrition: Calories: 334, Carbs: 42g, Fat: 17g, Protein: 5g

90. Strawberry Dalgona Coffee

Preparation time: 10 minutes
Cooking time: 7 minutes
Servings: 2

Ingredients:
- 8 oz strawberries, hulled & chopped
- 1/4 cup + 2 tbsp granulated sugar, divided
- 1/4 cup water
- 2 cups whole milk
- 2 tbsp coffee granules
- 2 tbsp water, boiling
- ice, as needed

Directions:

1. Place strawberries into your small saucepan, add 1/4 cup sugar plus 1/4 cup water and let it boil.
2. Adjust the heat to simmer, and often stir within 5-7 minutes until the liquid is reduced, plus strawberries are broken down.
3. Press the strawberries through your fine mesh strainer, and discard the strawberry solids. Let the syrup cool slightly, then mix into 2 cups of milk and keep aside.
4. Put the remaining 2 tbsp granulated sugar into your medium bowl. Add the 2 tbsp coffee granules plus 2 tbsp boiling water.
5. Whip the mixture using your hand mixer until fluffy. Keep aside.
6. Divide the strawberry milk between your two glasses, and add ice if you like. Spoon the whipped coffee mixture on top, and garnish with additional strawberries. Serve and enjoy!

Nutrition: Calories: 160, Carbs: 23g, Fat: 5g •Protein: 6g

91. Vegan Dalgona Coffee

Preparation time: 5 minutes
Cooking time: 0 minutes
Servings: 1

Ingredients:

- 2 tbsp hot water
- 2 tbsp coffee granules
- 2 tbsp coconut sugar
- 1 cup soymilk

Directions:

1. Mix the hot water, instant coffee, and coconut sugar into your small bowl, and whip within 2 minutes until it becomes a creamy and thick foam.
2. Fill your glass with ice, soymilk, and spoon 1/3 whipped coffee mixture on top. Serve and enjoy!

Nutrition: Calories: 80, Carbs: 19g, Fat: 0g, Protein: 0g

92. Honey & Vanilla Dalgona Coffee

Preparation time: 5 minutes
Servings: 2

Ingredients:

- 2 tbsp ground coffee
- 2 tbsp hot water
- 2 tbsp honey

For the honey vanilla latte:

- 2 cups milk
- 1 tsp vanilla extract
- 1 tsp honey

Directions:

1. Put the ground coffee, honey, plus hot water into your bowl, and whisk using an electric mixer until thick within 4 to 5 minutes.
2. Warm the milk plus honey until about to boil. Mix in the vanilla extract until well blended.
3. Divide this mixture into your glasses and serve with the whipped honey coffee mixture on top.

Nutrition: Calories: 140, Carbs: 12g, Fat: 8g, Protein: 10g

93. Coconut Dalgona Coffee

Preparation time: 5 minutes
Cooking time: 0 minutes
Servings: 1

Ingredients:

- 1 cup whole milk
- 1 tbsp sugar
- 2 tbsp shredded coconut
- 1 tbsp coffee granules
- ¼ cup water
- 4 ice cubes

Directions:

1. Whip the coffee granules, sugar, plus water in your bowl using a wire whisk until it thickens.
2. Pour the milk and shredded coconut into your blender and blend until smooth.
3. Pour the milk mixture into your glass with ice cubes
4. Top with the whipped coffee mixture. Serve and enjoy.

Nutrition: Calories: 227, Carbs: 24g, Fat: 11.3g, Protein: 8.2g

94. Chocolate Dalgona Coffee

Preparation time: 5 minutes
Cooking time: 0 minutes
Servings: 1

Ingredients:

- 1 cup whole milk
- 1 tbsp coffee granules
- 1 tbsp sugar
- ¼ cup water
- 2 tbsp cocoa powder
- 4 ice cubes

Directions:

1. Whip the coffee granules, sugar, plus water in your bowl using a wire whisk until it thickens.
2. Pour the milk plus cocoa powder into your blender and blend until smooth.
3. Pour the milk mixture into your glass with ice cubes
4. Top with the whipped coffee mixture. Serve and enjoy.

Nutrition: Calories 251, Fat 12.7g, Carbs 30.5g, Protein 10.2g

ESPRESSO DRINKS

95.   Bicerin Coffee

Preparation time: 5 minutes
Cooking time: 1 minute
Servings: 2

Ingredients:
- 1 cup milk
- 2 shots espresso
- 3 oz chocolate
- 4 tbsp whipped cream for topping

Directions:
1. Mix the milk plus chocolate in your saucepan until it boils. Keep whisking within 1 minute.
2. Fill 1/3 of your glass with this mixture, then pour the espresso shots. Top with whipped cream and serve.

Nutrition: Calories: 182, Carbs: 11g, Fat: 16g, Protein: 5g

96.   Espresso Macchiato

Preparation time: 5 minutes
Cooking time: 0 minutes
Servings: 1

Ingredients:
- 1 cup hot water
- 1 teaspoon ground espresso coffee
- 2 tbsp milk
- 2–3 tbsp hot milk

Directions:
1. Brew the espresso in your coffee machine. Add freshly brewed coffee to a glass and add hot milk. Stir.
2. Use a milk frother to whip up some milk and use the foam to decorate the glass.

Nutrition: Calories 28, Fat 0.9g, Carbs 2.3g, Protein 1.8g

97. Macadamia Mocha Espresso

Preparation time: 5 minutes
Cooking time: 0 minutes
Servings: 1

Ingredients:

- 2 shots of espresso
- 1-ounce macadamia nut syrup
- 1-ounce chocolate fudge syrup
- ½ cup steamed milk

Directions:

1. Take two shots of coffee in a glass. Add macadamia nut and chocolate fudge syrup.
2. Fill the glass with steamed milk, and top with cream or chocolate if desired.

Nutrition: Calories: 120, Carbs: 11g, Fat: 2g, Protein: 16g

98. Café Bombon

Preparation time: 5 minutes
Cooking time: 0 minutes
Servings: 1

Ingredients:

- 1 espresso shot
- 1 cup condensed milk

Directions:

1. Take one espresso shot in a glass.
2. Pour condensed milk carefully on top so that layers are not disturbed.

Nutrition: Calories: 151, Protein: 7.72 g, Fat: 8.03 g, Carbohydrates: 12.14 g

99. Cocoa Powder Espresso

Preparation time: 5 minutes
Cooking time: 0 minutes
Servings: 1

Ingredients:

- 1 tbsp cocoa powder
- 1 tsp powdered sugar
- ½ cup brewed coffee, hot
- ¼ cup whipped cream

Directions:

1. Take a serving glass and add the brewed coffee and cocoa powder and stir.
2. Use a mixer to whip the whipped cream and powdered sugar. Spoon the mixture over the coffee and serve.

Nutrition: Calories 111, Fat 10g, Carbs 6.3g, Protein 1.8g

100. Hazelnut Espresso

Preparation time: 5 minutes
Cooking time: 0 minutes
Servings: 1

Ingredients:

- 1 tbsp grated chocolate
- 1 tbsp hazelnut syrup
- 1 tsp ground espresso coffee
- ½ cup water
- ¼ cup milk

Directions:

1. Pour the brew espresso and milk into a serving glass and stir.
2. Now add the hazelnut syrup and stir.
3. Top with the grated chocolate and serve.

Nutrition: Calories 120, Fat 7.5g, Carbs 10.1g, Protein 3.5g

101.   Caramel & Apple Espresso

Preparation time: 10 minutes
Cooking time: 0 minutes
Servings: 1

Ingredients:

- 1 cup apple juice
- 1 tbsp powdered sugar
- ¼ cup heavy whipping cream
- 5 ice cubes
- 1 tbsp caramel sauce (for serving)
- ½ cup of cold espresso
- 3 tbsp caramel sauce
- Cinnamon

Directions:

1. Take a serving glass with ice and pour in the hot espresso, caramel sauce and apple juice. Mix.
2. Use a mixer to mix the whipped cream and powdered sugar and use the mixture to decorate the glass.
3. Complete by adding a pinch of cinnamon and the caramel sauce on top.

Nutrition: Calories 566, Fat 18g, Carbs 97.6g, Protein 4.9g

102.   Café Au Lait

Preparation time: 5 minutes
Cooking time: 0 minutes
Servings: 2

Ingredients:

- 1 cup warm milk
- 2 cup hot water
- 2 tbsp sugar
- 2 tsp cocoa powder for serving
- 4 tsp ground espresso coffee

Directions:

1. Make espresso with your coffee machine and pour it into a cup along with hot milk and sugar. Stir it all together until combined.
2. Top with the cocoa powder and serve.

Nutrition: Calories 112, Fat 2.8g, Carbs 19g, Protein 4.6g

103. Caramel Affogato

Preparation time: 5 minutes
Cooking time: 0 minutes
Servings: 1

Ingredients:

- ¼ cup warm milk
- 2 scoops of caramel ice cream
- 2 tsp finely ground espresso

Directions:

1. Make espresso coffee with your coffee machine and pour it into a container with the caramel ice cream.
2. Stir the coffee and ice cream until the latter has melted.
3. Add the mixture to a small cup with the hot milk, stir and serve.

Nutrition: Calories 352, Fat 17.3g, Carbs 45g, Protein 6.1g

104. Tembleque Latte

Preparation time: 5 minutes
Cooking time: 5 minutes
Servings: 1

Ingredients:

- 1 shot of brewed espresso
- 1 (1.5 fluid oz.) jigger coconut-flavored syrup
- 1/2 cup milk
- 1 pinch of ground cinnamon

Directions:

1. In a mug, mix coconut syrup with espresso. Pour the milk into your saucepan, then heat it at medium to low heat for around 5 minutes until it boils.
2. In the espresso mixture, stir the warm milk in. Finish off by sprinkling cinnamon into the latte.

Nutrition: Calories: 215, Carbohydrate: 44.3 g, Fat: 2.5 g, Protein: 4.1 g

105.   Almond Infused Espresso

Preparation time: 5 minutes
Cooking time: 0 minutes
Servings: 1

Ingredients:

- 1 tsp ground espresso coffee
- ½ tsp almond extract
- ¼ cup almond milk
- ¾ cup hot water

Directions:

1. Add the prepared espresso to a small cup with the almond extract and stir.
2. Now add the almond milk and stir again.

Nutrition: Calories 146, Fat 14.3g, Carbs 3.6g, Protein 1.6g

106.   Cloud Caramello Macchiato

Preparation time: 5 minutes
Cooking time: 0 minutes
Servings: 1

Ingredients:

- 1 tsp caramel sauce
- 1 tsp ground espresso coffee
- 1 tsp milk powder
- ½ tsp powdered sugar
- ¼ cup heavy whipping cream
- ¼ cup milk

Directions:

1. Brew the espresso with your coffee machine and pour it in a serving glass.
2. Take a bowl and pour in the milk, powdered milk, whipping cream and powdered sugar.
3. Mix the mixture with a hand mixer until you see "peaks" forming.
4. Add the mixture on top of the espresso and top everything with the caramel sauce.

Nutrition: Calories 168, Fat 12.4g, Carbs 11g, Protein 3.9g

107. Doppio Coffee

Preparation time: 5 minutes
Cooking time: 0 minutes
Servings: 1

Ingredients:

- ½ cup boiling water
- 1 tbsp ground espresso beans

Directions:

1. Mix boiling water with ground espresso in a cup.
2. When you notice the coffee is smooth, put the espresso in a serving glass and enjoy!

Nutrition: Calories 1, Fat 0g, Carbs 0g, Protein 0g

108. Birthday Frappuccino

Preparation time: 5 minutes
Cooking time: 0 minutes
Servings: 1

Ingredients:

- 2 tbsp hazelnut syrup
- ½ cup milk
- 1 tsp vanilla extract
- 6 cup ice cubes
- vanilla ice cream
- ½ cup espresso
- 1 tbsp sprinkles

Directions:

1. Brew the espresso with your coffee machine.
2. Mix the cold espresso, ice cubes, milk, vanilla extract and hazelnut syrup in a blender.
3. Place the mixture in a serving glass and top with the vanilla ice cream.
4. Add some sprinkles and serve.

Nutrition: Calories 468, Fat 25.2g, carbs 49.1g, Protein 10.1g

109. Cherry Iced Espresso

Preparation time: 5 minutes
Cooking time: 0 minutes
Servings: 1

Ingredients:

- 6 ice cubes
- ½ tsp vanilla extract
- 3 tbsp cherry syrup
- 1 cup espresso

Directions:

1. Brew the espresso with your coffee machine and let it cool down.

2. Pour the cold espresso in a serving glass with the ice cubes and vanilla extract.

3. Add the cherry syrup and mix until smooth.

Nutrition: Calories 203, Fat 0g, Carbs 48.3g, Protein 0.3g

110. Butterscotch Latte

Preparation time: 5 minutes
Cooking time: 0 minutes
Servings: 1

Ingredients:

- 2 tbsp butterscotch sauce
- ½ cup espresso
- 1 tbsp brown sugar
- Pinch of cinnamon
- ¼ cup cream
- 1 tbsp molasses
- ¼ cup heavy whipping cream

Directions:

1. Brew the espresso with your coffee machine.

2. Take a serving glass and add the espresso, butterscotch, molasses and whipping cream and mix.

3. With a hand mixer mix the whipping cream and the brown sugar and place on top of the serving glass. Top it with cinnamon and serve.

Nutrition: Calories 443, Fat 14.5g, Carbs 78.7g, Protein 1.9g

111. Pumpkin Espresso

Preparation time: 10 minutes
Cooking time: 7 minutes
Servings: 2

Ingredients:

- 4 cups milk
- 1 tbsp. pumpkin spice
- ¾ cup. pumpkin puree
- 1 tsp. vanilla extract
- Whipped cream, chocolate syrup for garnishing
- 2 cups espresso, brewed
- 5 tbsp. sugar
- 2 tsp. cinnamon
- 3 cups ice
-

Directions:

1. In a saucepan over medium heat, add espresso and milk, stir cook for 2 minutes. Then add sugar, vanilla, pumpkin puree, cinnamon, and pumpkin spice.
2. Continue cooking for 5 minutes. Remove from heat and allow to cool for 5 minutes.
3. Once cool, transfer the mixture to the blender and start blending.
4. Once all the ingredients are mixed, add ice and blend again until mixture become smooth and consistent.
5. Once done, transfer to the serving glass decorated with chocolate syrup and serve with whipped cream and chocolate syrup topping.

Nutrition: Calories: 100, Carbs: 9g, Fat: 5g, Protein: 3g

112. Avocado Espresso

Preparation time: 5 minutes
Servings: 1

Ingredients:

- ¼ cup espresso cooled
- 2 tbsp. condensed milk, sweetened
- ½ avocado
- 1 cup milk

Directions:

1. In a high-speed blender, add milk, condensed milk, espresso and avocado.
2. Blend until all the ingredients are mixed through and mixture becomes consistent.
3. Once ready, transfer to the serving glass. Drizzle of chocolate syrup on top and serve.

Nutrition: Calories: 150, Carbs: 32g, Fat: 3g, Protein: 0g

113. Café Americano

Preparation time: 5 minutes
Cooking time: 0 minutes
Servings: 1

Ingredients:

- 1 espresso shot
- 6 oz hot water

Directions:

1. Pour hot water into a cup, and pour an espresso shot into the hot water. Serve and enjoy!

Nutrition: Calories: 10, Carbs: 2g, Fat: 10g, Protein: 0g

114. Choco Keto-Coffee Milkshake

Preparation time: 5 minutes
Cooking time: 0 minutes
Servings: 2

Ingredients:

- 2 tsp. espresso powder
- 4 tsp. cocoa
- 4 oz almond milk, unsweetened
- 1 tbsp. avocado oil
- 2 tbsp. erythritol sweetener
- 3 oz coconut milk, unsweetened
- ¾ cup water
- 1 ½ cups ice cubes

Directions:

1. In a blender, add espresso powder, cocoa, almond milk, erythritol sweetener, coconut milk and ice cubes.
2. Blend until all the ingredients are mixed through, gradually add water until desired consistency is achieved.
3. Once ready, transfer to the serving glasses and serve.

Nutrition: Calories: 275, Carbs: 8g, Fat: 27g, Protein: 3g

115. Red Eye Coffee Espresso

Preparation time: 15 minutes
Cooking time: 0 minutes
Servings: 1

Ingredients:

- 1 espresso shot
- 2/3 cup regular brewed coffee

Directions:

1. Take a single shot of espresso. Take brewed coffee in a demitasse cup.
2. Pour the shot of espresso in it, and serve!

Nutrition: Calories: 4, Protein: 0.22 g, Fat: 0.08 g, Carbohydrates: 0.48 g

116. Creamed Belgian Coffee

Preparation time: 5 minutes
Cooking time: 0 minutes
Servings: 1

Ingredients:

- 2 shots espresso
- 1 fl. oz. Belgian cookie syrup
- 2 oz. whipped cream
- Dark chocolate, grated

Directions:

1. In a serving cup, stir together the espresso and Belgian cookie syrup.
2. Serve with whipped cream and dark chocolate on top.

Nutrition: Calories: 188, Fat: 17.4 g, Carbohydrates: 1.9 g, Protein: 1.1 g

MILK RECIPES

117.   Pecan-Maple Latte

Preparation time: 10 minutes
Cooking time: 5 minutes
Servings: 1

Ingredients:

For the Syrup:

- 1/4 cup natural peanut butter
- 1/4 cup maple syrup
- 2 tbsp brown sugar
- 1/2 tbsp unsalted butter
- 1/3 cup heavy cream
- 1 tsp pure vanilla extract,

For the Latte:

- 1 shot espresso
- 2 tbsp pecan-maple syrup
- 1/2 cup steamed milk,

For the Garnishing:

- Whipped cream, as you like
- chopped pecans, toasted, as you like

Directions:

1. In a small pot over medium-high heat, add maple syrup, peanut butter, brown sugar and butter. Stir while cooking for 2 to3 minutes until sugar disappears and dissolves completely.
2. Remove the syrup from the heat, add vanilla extract and cream, set aside until completely cooled. This syrup is enough for eight lattes.
3. In a mug, add espresso and 2 tbsp. of pecan-maple syrup, mix until blended thoroughly.
4. Then add steamed milk, top with the whipped cream and pecans, and serve.

Nutrition: Calories: 160, Carbs: 28g, Fat: 5g, Protein: 1g

118.   Iced Ube Milky Coffee

Preparation time: 10 minutes
Servings: 5-6

Ingredients:

- 16 oz. almond milk
- 16 oz. rice milk
- 1/4 cup granulated sugar
- Ice, crushed, for mixing and serving
- 16 oz. coconut milk
- 2 tsp ground cinnamon
- 3 tsp ube (yam) extract
- 1 shot Espresso

Directions:

1. In a large pitcher, pour milk, then gradually add sugar and cinnamon, keep mixing quickly to avoid forming.

2. Once everything is mixed through, add ube extract, and mix until blended completely.

3. Pour some ice in the serving glass, add ube mixture until nearly full, and serve with 1 shot of espresso on top.

Nutrition: Calories: 158, Carbs: 37g, Fat: 0g, Protein: 2g

119.   Breakfast Coffee Milk

Preparation time: 10 minutes
Servings: 6

Ingredients:

- 4 cups whole milk
- 1/2 cup maple syrup
- 2 tsp baking cocoa
- 1 & 1/3 cups strong brewed coffee
- 2 tbsp pure molasses

For the Whipped Cream:

- 1 cup heavy whipping cream
- 1 tbsp pure vanilla extract
- 1 tbsp maple syrup
- Extra baking cocoa

Directions:

1. In a saucepan over medium heat, add milk, coffee, maple syrup, molasses and baking cocoa. Stir occasionally and bring the mixture to barely simmering, remove from heat.

2. In a small bowl, add cream and beat until it begins to thick. Add vanilla and maple syrup, continue beating until it starts making soft peaks.

3. Once ready, transfer the coffee milk to the serving glass. Serve with whipped cream and dust with extra cocoa on top.

120. Coffee Vanilla Milkshake

Preparation time: 5 minutes
Cooking time: 0 minutes
Servings: 1

Ingredients:

- 2 scoops of vanilla ice cream, divided
- 2 shots of espresso, cooled
- 2/3 cup skim milk
- 5-6 cubes of ice

Directions:

1. In a high-speed blender, add 1 scoop of ice cream, espresso, skim milk, and ice. Blend until mixture becomes consistent and smooth.

2. Once done, pour the blended coffee mixture into a chilled serving glass. Serve with the reserved scoop of ice cream on top.

Nutrition: Calories: 224, Carbs: 51.1g, Fat: 2.9g, Protein: 2.8g

121. Soy Milk Coffee Crumble Frappe

Preparation time: 5 minutes
Cooking time: 0 minutes
Servings: 2

Ingredients:

- 1 cup soy milk, unsweetened
- 1 cup strong brewed coffee
- 1/4 cup cashew nuts
- 1/4 cup cacao nibs
- 2 tbsp sugar-free syrup
- 10 ice cubes

Directions:

1. In a blender, add brewed coffee, soy milk, cacao nibs, cashew nuts, sugar-free syrup, and ice.

2. Blend the mixture until desired consistency is achieved.

3. Once ready, divide the mixture into 2 chilled tall glasses. Add some cacao nibs on top and serve.

Nutrition: Calories: 255, Fat: 6.4 g, Carbohydrate: 40.1 g, Protein: 8.1 g

122.   Irish Coffee Milkshake

Preparation time: 5 minutes
Cooking time: 0 minutes
Servings: 1

Ingredients:

- 2 tsp sugar
- ½ cup low-fat yogurt
- 1 tsp Irish whiskey
- ½ cup milk
- 1 tsp coffee granules
- Ice cubes, as needed

Directions:

1. In a blender, add sugar, milk, yogurt, coffee granules, whiskey and ice.
2. Blend all the ingredients on low speed for 60 seconds.
3. Once desired smoothness is achieved, transfer to the serving glass with extra ice cubes and serve!

Nutrition: Calories: 228, Carbs: 10g, Fat: 9g, Protein: 1g

123.   White Chocolate Latte

Preparation time: 5 minutes
Cooking time: 10 minutes
Servings: 2

Ingredients:

- 1 1/2 cups milk
- 1/8 tsp vanilla extract
- 1/2 cup brewed espresso
- 1 tbsp heavy cream
- 1 tbsp white sugar
- 1/4 cup white chocolate chips, chopped

Directions:

1. In a saucepan over high heat, add cream and milk. Whisk until mixture becomes frothy and hot. Then remove from the heat; add vanilla and sugar, mix thoroughly.
2. In a mug, add white chocolate chips and hot espresso, whisk until smooth, and transfer half into another cup.
3. Pour in frothy hot milk and stir to blend with flavoring, serve immediately.

Nutrition: Calories: 270, Carbohydrate: 27.7 g, Fat: 14.4 g, Protein: 7.8 g

124.   Minty White Mocha Frappe

Preparation time: 5 minutes
Servings: 2

Ingredients:

- 3 shots espresso
- 4 tbsp sugar-free white chocolate syrup
- 10-12 ice cubes
- Cubed chocolate wafer bars to serve
- 1 cup skim milk
- 2 tbsp sugar-free peppermint syrup
- Whipped cream to serve

Directions:

1. In a high-speed blender, add skim milk, espresso, peppermint syrup, white chocolate syrup, and ice cubes. Blend until consistent and smooth.
2. Once ready, transfer to 2 chilled glasses. Top with some whipped cream, garnish with cubed chocolate wafer bars and serve.

Nutrition: Calories: 353, Fat: 13.8 g, Carbohydrate: 48.1 g, Protein: 6.8 g

125.   Caramel Milk Latte

Preparation time: 5 minutes
Cooking time: 6 minutes
Servings: 1

Ingredients:

- 2 oz espresso
- 2 tbsp caramel sauce, + more for drizzling
- 10 oz milk
- 1 tbsp sugar (optional)

Directions:

1. Pour the espresso into your mug.
2. Pour milk in a saucepan over medium heat, allow to heat for 5 minutes until just starts to boil.
3. Then add sugar and caramel sauce to the sauce pan and whisk until blended.
4. Make froth using a frother for 25 to 30 seconds.
5. Spin your glass, gently tap on the counter until large bubbles appear.
6. Hold back foam using the back of a spoon, and add milk into your espresso. Top the coffee with remaining foam, drizzle caramel sauce and serve.

126.   Date & Banana Coffee Smoothie

Preparation time: 5 minutes
Cooking time: 0 minutes
Servings: 1

Ingredients:

- 4 pitted dates
- ½ cup of fresh coffee
- ¼ tsp vanilla extract
- 1 frozen banana, peeled, chopped & freeze overnight
- ½ cup soya milk

Directions:

1. In a blender, add dates, frozen banana, soya milk, coffee, and vanilla extract.
2. Blend until smooth, transfer to your glass and serve.

Nutrition: Calories: 170, Carbs: 0g, Fat: 5g, Protein: 0g

127.   Lavender Coffee Milk Latte

Preparation time: 5 minutes
Cooking time: 5 minutes
Servings: 1

Ingredients:

- 2 oz espresso
- 1 tsp culinary-grade lavender buds
- 10 oz milk
- 1 tsp honey, plus more as needed

Directions:

1. Transfer the espresso into a mug.
2. In a saucepan over moderate heat, add honey, milk and lavender. Heat for 4 to 5 minutes until start to simmer.
3. Remove from heat and strain into a glass jar. Remove the lavender buds and discard.
4. Make froth using a frother for around 30 seconds.
5. Spin your glass, gently tap on the counter until large bubbles appear.
6. Hold back foam using the back of a spoon, and add milk into your espresso. Top the coffee with remaining foam, and serve.

Nutrition: Calories: 100, Carbs: 17g, Fat: 2g, Protein: 2g

128. Vanilla Milk Espresso Frappe

Preparation time: 5 minutes
Cooking time: 0 minutes
Servings: 1

Ingredients:

- 2 oz chilled espresso
- 1 cup ice
- ¼ tsp vanilla extract
- 1 cup vanilla ice cream
- 4 oz milk
- Whipped cream, for garnish

Directions:

1. Combine the espresso, ice cream, ice, milk, plus vanilla in your blender, and blend until smooth.

2. Serve topped with whipped cream, as desired.

Nutrition: Calories: 471, Carbs: 69g, Fat: 14g, Protein: 16g

129. Cinnamon & Honey Latte

Preparation time: 5 minutes
Cooking time: 5 minutes
Servings: 1

Ingredients:

- 2 oz espresso
- 2 tsp honey, + more for garnish
- ½ tsp vanilla extract
- ¼ tsp ground cinnamon, + more for garnish
- 10 oz milk

Directions:

1. Transfer the espresso into a mug, add vanilla, honey and ground cinnamon, mix well.

2. Pour milk in your saucepan over moderate heat. Remove just before milk starts to boil.

3. Make froth using a frother for around 20 to 30 seconds.

4. Twist your glass and gently tap on the counter until large bubbles start to appear.

5. Hold back foam using the back of a spoon, and add milk into your espresso. Top the coffee with remaining foam, cinnamon and honey, serve immediately.

Nutrition: Calories: 155, Carbs: 27g, Fat: 4g, Protein: 4g

130. Almond Milk Choco Latte

Preparation time: 5 minutes
Cooking time: 0 minutes
Servings: 1

Ingredients:

- 2 shots of brewed espresso
- 1/2 tbsp chocolate-hazelnut spread
- 1/2 cup skim milk
- 1/4 cup almond milk creamer
- ice cubes, as needed

Directions:

1. Mix the chocolate-hazelnut spread and hot espresso in your cup, mix well until melted. Cover and refrigerate for 30 minutes.
2. Then add the almond milk creamer, ice and skim milk, mix thoroughly and serve.

Nutrition: Calories: 181, Carbohydrate: 26.5 g, Fat: 6.4 g, Protein: 4.7 g

COFFEE COCKTAILS

131. Chocolate Coffee Martini

Preparation time: 5 minutes
Cooking time: 0 minutes
Servings: 1

Ingredients:

- 1 tbsp vodka
- 2 ½ tbsp Bailey's Irish Cream liqueur
- 1 scoop of chocolate ice cream
- 2 tbsp chocolate liqueur
- 4 tbsp cold-brewed coffee

Directions:

1. Pour the Irish Cream into your martini glass, add chocolate liqueur followed by the vodka.

2. Finally add coffee to create a beautiful layer with the mixture. Top with the ice cream, and serve.

Nutrition: Calories: 341, Carbs: 33g, Fat: 8g, Protein: 2g

132. Flame Coffee

Preparation time: 5 minutes
Cooking time: 0 minutes
Servings: 2

Ingredients:

- 1-1/2 tsp butter
- Dash each ground cinnamon, nutmeg & cloves
- 3 oz. Cognac or brandy
- 2 tbsps. packed brown sugar
- 1/8 tsp vanilla extract
- 4 orange peel strips (about 1-3 inches)
- 2 cups strong brewed coffee
- Cinnamon sticks and sweetened whipped cream, optional, as you like

Directions:

1. Dissolve the butter in your small skillet over medium-low heat. Add in spices, orange peel and vanilla; stir well

2. Take away from the heat; add Cognac. Take the pan back to the heat; ignite the Cognac mixture carefully.

3. Extinguish the flames by gradually pouring over with brewed coffee. Remove orange peel and discard; add in brown sugar and stir till blended. Transfer into mugs.

4. Add whipped cream and cinnamon sticks (if desired), then serve immediately.

Nutrition: Calories: 153, Carbohydrate: 14 g, Fat: 3 g, Protein: 0 g

133.   Colorado Bulldog Cocktail

Preparation time: 5 minutes
Cooking time: 0 minutes
Servings: 1

Ingredients:

- 1 oz vodka
- 1 oz light cream or milk
- 1 oz coffee liqueur
- 1 to 2 ounces cola, to taste

Directions:

1. Pour the vodka plus coffee liqueur into your old-fashioned glass filled with ice.

2. Add the cream and top with cola. Stir well and serve immediately.

Nutrition: Calories: 304, Carbs: 15g, Fat: 5g, Protein: 4g

134.   Brazilian Iced Coffee Cocktail

Preparation time: 5 minutes
Cooking time: 0 minutes
Servings: 1

Ingredients:

- Ice cubes, for serving, as needed
- 2 oz coconut rum, such as Malibu
- 1 tsp sugar
- 4 oz espresso or strong coffee
- 2 oz heavy (whipping) cream

Directions:

1. Fill your glass with some ice and keep it aside.

2. First pour ice in a cocktail shaker, then add rum, espresso, sugar and heavy cream. Cover the cocktail shaker and shake briskly for 10 to 15 seconds.

3. Transfer the drink to the glass with ice and serve.

Nutrition: Calories: 126, Carbs: 18g, Fat: 5g, Protein: 3g

135. Irish Whiskey Coffee

Preparation time: 5 minutes
Cooking time: 0 minutes
Servings: 2

Ingredients:

- 1 (1.5 oz.) jigger Irish cream liqueur
- 1 cup hot brewed coffee
- 1 dash ground nutmeg
- 1 (1.5 oz.) jigger Irish whiskey
- 1 tbsp whipped cream

Directions:

1. Combine the Irish cream with Irish whiskey in your coffee mug.

2. Pour a dash of nutmeg, brewed coffee plus a dab of whipped cream on top. Serve and enjoy!

Nutrition: Calories: 462, Carbs: 56g, Fat: 23g, Protein: 5g

136. Amaretto Iced Coffee

Preparation time: 10 minutes
Cooking time: 0 minutes
Servings: 8

Ingredients:

- 4 cups of strong brewed coffee
- 1/2 cup amaretto
- 1/4 cup + 3 tbsp sugar, divided
- 2/3 cup heavy whipping cream

Directions:

1. Whisk amaretto, ¼ cup of sugar and coffee in a bowl and leave to cool.

2. Once cool enough, transfer to an 8" square dish, place in a freezer and leave until completely frozen, stir after every 30 minutes.

3. Meanwhile, beat cream in a small bowl till it begins to thicken. Add the leftover sugar, then beat till it forms stiff peaks. Cover and leave in the refrigerator until serving.

4. Remove frozen coffee mixture from freezer, take a scoop out and transfer to the serving glass. Add whipped cream on top and serve immediately.

Nutrition: Calories: 218, Carbs: 26g, Fat: 6g, Protein: 1g

137. Bavarian Coffee Cocktail

Preparation time: 5 minutes
Cooking time: 0 minutes
Servings: 1

Ingredients:

- 4 oz coffee
- ½ oz mint schnapps
- Whipped cream, for garnish
- ½ oz coffee-flavored liqueur, such as Kahlúa
- 1 tsp sugar

Directions:

1. Pour the coffee into your mug, then stir in the coffee-flavored liqueur, mint schnapps, plus sugar.
2. Serve topped with whipped cream, as desired.

Nutrition: Calories: 20, Carbs: 3g, Fat: 1g, Protein: 0g

138. Iced Coffee Margarita

Preparation time: 5 minutes
Cooking time: 0 minutes
Servings: 2

Ingredients:

- 1 tbsp. honey
- 1 tbsp. coffee beans, ground
- 2 shots tequila
- 1 tbsp. white sugar
- 2 cups of cold coffee
- 2 lemon twists (lemon rind)

Directions:

1. In a plate, add sugar and coffee. Mix well. In another bowl, add honey.
2. Dip the serving glass first in honey and then in the sugar and coffee mixture so that the rims of the glass are covered with the mixture.
3. Add ice into the glass, and pour half with tequila.
4. Pour coffee to fill the glass.
5. Garnish with lemon twists and serve.

Nutrition: Calories: 226, Carbs: 22g, Fat: 0g, Protein: 0g

139. Chilean Long-Tail Monkey Punch

Preparation time: 15 minutes
Servings: 16

Ingredients:

- 3 cinnamon sticks, 3" each
- 4 cups low fat milk, 2%
- ½ cup brandy
- 2 tsp. vanilla extract
- 2 cups of coffee, strongly brewed
- 1 cup of sugar
- 3 cloves, whole

Directions:

1. In a saucepan over medium heat, add cinnamon, milk, cloves and sugar. Bring the mixture to boil.

2. Then reduce heat and allow to simmer for 4 to 5 minutes. Remove from heat and allow to cool until it reaches room temperature.

3. Strain the mixture into a large jug and discard the spices. Then add brandy, coffee and vanilla, cover and allow to chill in the freezer. Once ready, transfer to the serving glass and serve chilled.

Nutrition: Calories: 64, Carbs: 14g, Fat: 0g, Protein: 0g

140. Celtic Coffee

Preparation time: 10 minutes
Servings: 1

Ingredients:

- 1 egg white
- 1/2 tsp stevia powder, or to taste
- 3 tbsp coarsely ground coffee beans
- 2 tbsp Scotch whiskey
- 1 tsp lemon juice
- 1/4 tsp grated lemon zest, or to taste
- 1 cup boiling water
- 2 tsp honey

Directions:

1. Beat egg white using electric mixer until soft peaks are formed. Add stevia powder, lemon zest and juice, mix well.

2. Pour boiling water in a French press, add coffee, cover and allow it to steep for 3 to 5 minutes.

3. In a glass, combine Scotch and honey, then stir in coffee; mix well. Place lemon-flavored egg white on top and serve.

141.   Orange & Coffee Martini

Preparation time: 5 minutes
Cooking time: 0 minutes
Servings: 1

Ingredients:

- Ice cubes, as needed
- 2 oz. strong brewed coffee, cooled
- 1 oz. vodka
- ½ oz. orange liqueur
- ½ oz. hazelnut liqueur

Directions:

1. Fill ¾ of a tumbler or a mixing glass with ice cubes. Add brewed coffee, vodka, orange liqueur and hazelnut liqueur, mix until condensation forms on the glass's outer side.
2. In a chilled cocktail glass, strain the drink, then immediately serve.

Nutrition: Calories: 172, Carbohydrate: 13 g, Fat: 0 g, Protein: 0 g

142.   Minty Choco Martini

Preparation time: 5 minutes
Cooking time: 0 minutes
Servings: 1

Ingredients:

- 5 ice cubes
- 2 tbsp vodka
- 2 tbsp chocolate-mint cocktail mix
- 1 tbsp Kahlua or coffee-flavored tequila or any other coffee liqueur
- 1 tbsp brewed coffee

Directions:

1. Add ice cubes, cocktail mix, vodka, tequila and coffee in a cocktail shaker. Shake until water starts condensing on the outside of the cocktail shaker.
2. Strain the mixture in a martini glass. Serve with a green martini umbrella or with decorative mint leaves.

Nutrition: Calories: 80, Carbs: 19g, Fat: 0g, Protein: 0g

143. Ginger Coffee Cocktail

Preparation time: 10 minutes
Cooking time: 30 minutes
Servings: 1-2

Ingredients:

- 3 ice cubes
- 1 cup water
- 4 tbsp coffee-flavored tequila
- 1 cup semi-packed brown sugar
- 1 sliced ginger, peeled
- 1 gingerbread, finely crushed

Directions:

1. In a saucepan over medium heat, pour water, add ginger and sugar, and bring the mixture to boil. Then remove from heat, strain the ginger, and let the mixture cool. Once cool, transfer to freezer and allow to chill for 30 minutes.
2. Transfer the chilled mixture to the cocktail shaker, pour in tequila and shake vigorously. Strain the cocktail in a small glass.
3. Top with the crushed gingerbread. Serve on the rocks.

Nutrition: Calories: 211, Carbs: 16g, Fat: 10g, Protein: 6g

144. K.O. Coffee

Preparation time: 5 minutes
Cooking time: 0 minutes
Servings: 3

Ingredients:

- 2 cups of cold coffee
- 1 cup milk
- 1/4 cup white chocolate chips
- 2 tbsp caramel syrup
- 2 tbsp coffee-flavored liqueur (such as Kahlua®)
- 1 tbsp real maple syrup
- 1/4 cup chocolate-covered espresso beans
- 16 ice cubes
- 1/4 cup semisweet chocolate chips
- 2 tbsp chocolate syrup
- 2 tbsp hazelnut liqueur
- 2 tbsp confectioners' sugar
- 2 scoops of vanilla ice cream

Directions:

1. In a large blender, combine maple syrup, confectioners' sugar, coffee-flavored liqueur, hazelnut liqueur, caramel syrup, chocolate syrup, white chocolate chips, semisweet chocolate chips, milk, ice, and coffee. Briefly blend till combined. Add ice cream, then blend till smooth.

2. To suck up the espresso beans, add a wide straw. Add espresso beans and pour the coffee drink on top into a serving glass. Serve.

Nutrition: Calories: 472, Carbohydrate: 67.7 g, Fat: 18 g, Protein: 5.9 g

145. Hot Baja Coffee

Preparation time: 10 minutes
Cooking time: 3 hours
Servings: 8

Ingredients:

- 8 cups of hot water
- ¾ cup whipped cream
- ¼ cup crème de cacao
- 2 tbsp grated chocolate
- ½ cup coffee liqueur
- 3 tbsp coffee granules

Directions:

1. In your saucepan, pour the coffee granules plus hot water. Add the crème de cacao plus coffee liqueurs and stir it well.

2. Place the saucepan over low heat, and cover it with a lid within 3 hours. Remove and garnish with the whipped cream plus grated chocolate. Serve immediately.

Nutrition: Calories: 112, Fat 2.89g, Carbs 15.04g, Protein 0.95g

146. Café Royale

Preparation time: 5 minutes
Cooking time: 0 minutes
Servings: 1

Ingredients:

- 4 tsp brandy
- 2 cubes sugar
- 1 cup of hot coffee

Directions:

1. Pour the hot coffee into your cup, and carefully drop 2 tsp. brandy on top to make them float.
2. Pour 2 tbsp. brandy and dissolve the sugar cubes in it.
3. Place the teaspoon above the cup, carefully ignite the contents of the teaspoon, and pour slowly. Let it cool and serve.

Nutrition: Calories: 157, Carbs: 3g, Fat: 9g, Protein: 15g

147. Kahlua Coffee

Preparation time: 10 minutes
Cooking time: 3-4 hours
Servings: 8

Ingredients:

- 2 quarts of hot water
- 1/2 cup Kahlua (coffee liqueur)
- 1/4 cup creme de cacao
- 3 tbsp coffee granules
- 2 cups heavy whipping cream
- 1/4 cup sugar
- 1 tsp vanilla extract
- 2 tbsp grated semisweet chocolate

Directions:

1. Combine creme de cacao, coffee granules, Kahlua and water in a 4-quart slow cooker over low heat. Cover and cook for0 3 to 4 hours until heated through.
2. Beat cream in a big bowl till it begins to thicken. Beat vanilla and sugar in till it forms soft peaks. Serve chocolate and whipped cream together with the warm coffee.

Nutrition: Calories: 200, Carbs: 30g, Fat: 0g, Protein: 0g

148. Rum Flavored Ice Coffee

Preparation time: 5 minutes
Cooking time: 0 minutes
Servings: 1

Ingredients:

- 1 cup espresso, cold brewed
- 3 tbsp. cream
- 2 tbsp. brown sugar
- 5 ice cubes
- 1 tbsp. rum, dark

Directions:

1. Pour ice in serving glass, then add cream, cold espresso, rum and brown sugar.

2. Mix until the brown sugar dissolves completely. Serve immediately.

Nutrition: Calories 128, Fat 2g, Carbs 18.8g, Protein 0.6g

149. Dalgona Coffee Cocktail

Preparation time: 5 minutes
Cooking time: 0 minutes
Servings: 1

Ingredients:

- 2 tbsp coffee powder
- 4 tbsp hot water
- 2 oz cream or coffee liqueur
- Ice, as needed
- 2 tbsp brown sugar
- 2 oz vodka
- 2 oz heavy cream
-

Directions:

1. In your medium-large bowl, add the coffee, brown sugar, plus hot water, and whip using your hand mixer until fluffy within 4 minutes on high speed.

2. In a cocktail shaker, add cream liqueur, vodka, ice cubes and heavy cream. Shake briskly for 8 to 10 seconds.

3. Once ready, transfer to serving glass, carefully top with whipped coffee mixture and serve.

Nutrition: Calories: 211, Carbs: 16g, Fat: 10g, Protein: 6g

150. Espresso Tonic

Preparation time: 5 minutes
Cooking time: 0 minutes
Servings: 1

Ingredients:

- 3 ½ oz tonic water
- ½ tsp orange extract
- 1 shot of light-medium espresso
- Dried or candied orange peel to garnish

Directions:

1. Put a few ice cubes to your mug or glass. Pour the orange extract and tonic water into the tumbler, and give it a light stir.

2. Pour the espresso crefully into the glass off of the back of a spoon, creating the cool effect where the coffee floats on top of the water. Drop your orange peel inside, and serve.

Nutrition: Calories: 95, Carbs: 23g, Fat: 0g, Protein: 0g

151. Praline Coffee

Preparation time: 10 minutes
Cooking time: 0 minutes
Servings: 3

Ingredients:

- 3 cups of hot black coffee
- 3/4 cup sugar
- 3/4 cup Praline liqueur
- 3/4 cup half-and-half milk
- 2 tbsp butter or margarine
- whipped cream, as needed

Directions:

1. Mix half and half milk, black coffee, sugar, plus butter in a saucer. Put on medium heat while stirring until about to boil.

2. Add the Praline liqueur to the mixture and stir further. Once ready, transfer to your coffee mugs, add whipped cream on top and serve immediately.

Nutrition: Calories: 55, Carbs: 7g, Fat: 3g, Protein: 0g

152.   Vienna Coffee

Preparation time: 10 minutes
Cooking time: 3 hours
Servings: 2

Ingredients:

- 2 cups brewed coffee
- 1 tbsp chocolate syrup
- Sugar as per taste
- ½ cup whipped cream
- 2 tbsp Irish cream liqueur

Directions:

1. Add the sugar, coffee, and chocolate syrup to your slow cooker. Cover and leave on low heat for 2 to 2 ½ hours.

2. Mix in the heavy cream plus Irish cream liqueur, and continue to cook again for another half hour. Garnish with whipped cream before serving.

Nutrition: Calories: 58, Carbs: 9g, Fat: 2g, Protein: 0g

153.   Cappuccino Royale

Preparation time: 5 minutes
Cooking time: 5 minutes
Servings: 2

Ingredients:

- 2 tbsp full of brandy
- 2 tbsp dark crème de cacao
- ½ a cup of freshly brewed espresso coffee
- 2 tbsp full of white rum
- ½ a cup of half-and-half milk
- Sugar, as needed

Directions:

1. Pour the freshly brewed espresso coffee into 2 cups.

2. Whisk the half-and-half milk in your bowl, and pour into your saucepan over low heat within a few minutes until it is frothy

3. Add 1 tbsp. white brandy, rum, plus crème de cacao to each espresso coffee cup.

4. Whisk the half and half milk again and pour into the cups. Add sugar as needed and serve.

Nutrition: Calories: 136, Carbs: 19g, Fat: 6g, Protein: 1g

154.   Coffee Nudge

Preparation time: 10 minutes
Cooking time: 0 minutes
Servings: 8

Ingredients:

- 8 cups of hot brewed coffee
- 8 fluid oz coffee-flavored liqueur
- 8 fluid oz brandy
- 4 fluid oz creme de cacao
- 2 cups whipped cream, garnish
- 2 tbsp chocolate sprinkles

Directions:

1. Pour 1 oz coffee liqueur and 1 oz brandy into the bottom of 8 coffee mugs. Add in ½ oz of each creme de cacao.
2. Fill hot coffee into each cup; add chocolate sprinkles and a dollop of whipped cream as garnish. Serve and enjoy!

Nutrition: Calories: 130, Carbs: 13g, Fat: 2g, Protein: 0g

155.   Mexican Coffee Cocktail

Preparation time: 5 minutes
Cooking time: 0 minutes
Servings: 1

Ingredients:

- 1 oz coffee-flavored liqueur
- 1/2 oz tequila
- 5 oz hot coffee
- 2 tbsp whipped cream

Directions:

1. In your coffee cup, add coffee liqueur and tequila, mix thoroughly.
2. Then add coffee, top with whipped cream and serve!

Nutrition: Calories: 155. Carbohydrate: 12 g, Fat: 1.4 g, Protein: 0.2 g

156.   Black Russian Coffee

Preparation time: 5 minutes
Cooking time: 0 minutes
Servings: 1

Ingredients:

- 4 tbsp vodka
- Ice, for serving, as needed
- 2 tbsp coffee-flavored liqueur
- For the garnish: cocktail cherry (optional)

Directions:

1. Add ice to the serving glass and set aside. Add the coffee-flavored liqueur and vodka to your mixing glass with ice, and stir until cold and blended.
2. Strain and pour the drink into serving glass. Garnish with a cocktail cherry on top. Stir lightly and enjoy.

Nutrition: Calories: 229, Carbs: 15g, Fat: 0g, Protein: 0g

157.   Chocolate Coffee Kiss

Preparation time: 5 minutes
Cooking time: 0 minutes
Servings:

Ingredients:

- 3/4 oz coffee liqueur
- 1/2 oz creme de cacao liqueur
- 1 cup hot brewed coffee
- 1 1/2 fluid oz. chocolate syrup
- 3/4 oz Irish cream liqueur
- 1 tsp. brandy-based orange liqueur (such as Grand Marnier®)
- 2 tbsp whipped cream
- 1 maraschino cherry

Directions:

1. Mix the creme de cacao, Grand Marnier, Irish cream, and coffee liqueur in a coffee mug. Fill hot coffee in the mug.
2. Spoon whipped cream on top. Drizzle chocolate syrup and garnish with maraschino cherry.

Nutrition: Calories: 132, Carbs: 12g, Fat: 9g, Protein: 4g

158. Frozen Almond Cocktail

Preparation time: 10 minutes
Cooking time: 0 minutes
Servings: 2

Ingredients:

- 1/2 cup milk
- 2 1/2 tbsp amaretto liqueur
- 1 cup vanilla ice cream
- 2 tbsp coffee-flavored liqueur
- 1/4 cup chocolate-flavored syrup
- 1 cup crushed ice

Directions:

1. Combine amaretto liqueur, chocolate-flavored syrup, coffee-flavored liqueur and milk in a blender. Stir in ice cream. Start blending and gradually add until consistent.

2. Add more ice cream or milk if the mixture gets too thin or too thick. Once ready, transfer to tall glasses, take 2 straws and serve.

Nutrition: Calories: 167, Carbs: 5g, Fat: 15g, Protein: 6g

159. Coffee Mcavee

Preparation time: 15 minutes
Cooking time: 0 minutes
Servings: 10

Ingredients:

- 5 cups vanilla ice cream
- 11 (1.5 oz) jiggers' coffee-flavored liqueur
- 1/4 cup white sugar
- 5 cups of hot brewed coffee
- 10 (1.5 oz) jiggers 151 proof rum

Directions:

1. In one saucer, add 2 jiggers of coffee-flavored liqueur. In another saucer, sprinkle sugar. Dip the rim of each glass first in the liqueur, then into sugar.

2. Into each glass, add 1 jigger of rum. Using a long match, set the rum on fire and let it burn around the glass's rim for about 60 seconds till it becomes caramel.

3. Use a ½ cup-sized scoop of ice cream to extinguish the fire in each glass. Pour over the ice cream with 1 jigger of coffee liqueur. Top with hot coffee and serve.

Nutrition: Calories: 100, Carbs: 16g, Fat: 3g, Protein: 4g

160. Godiva Irish Coffee

Preparation time: 5 minutes
Cooking time: 0 minutes
Servings: 1

Ingredients:

- 4 oz hot coffee
- ¾ oz Irish cream liqueur
- 1 ½ oz Godiva liqueur
- Whipped cream, as needed

Directions:

1. Pour the hot coffee into a desired coffee mug, and stir in the Irish cream liqueur plus Godiva liqueur.
2. Top with whipped cream and serve.

Nutrition: Calories: 228, Carbs: 10g, Fat: 9g, Protein: 1g

OTHER COFFEE RECIPES

161.   Vietnamese Egg Coffee

Preparation time: 5 minutes
Cooking time: 0 minutes
Servings: 1

Ingredients:

- 1 cup coffee, hot brewed
- 1 egg yolk
- 2 tbsp. sugar

Directions:

1. In a serving cup, pour brewed coffee, then add sugar and egg yolk.
2. Mix thoroughly until combined, and serve immediately.

Nutrition: Calories 146, Fat 4.6g, Carbs 24.6g, Protein 3g

162.   Continental Coffee Cooler

Preparation time: 15 minutes
Cooking time: 0 minutes
Servings: 4

Ingredients:

- 1-1/2 cups freshly brewed, French roast coffee
- ½ tsp Angostura bitters
- ½ tsp pure vanilla extract
- 1-1/2 tbsp sugar
- 1 cup cold club soda
- 4 orange sections

Directions:

1. Mix the coffee, vanilla, bitters, plus sugar, and pour into 4 (10-ounce) glasses.
2. Fill the glass with ice cubes. Add club soda on top and garnish with orange section.

Nutrition: Calories 25, Fat 0g, Carbs 6g, Protein 0g

163. Hong Kong Style Milk Coffee Tea

Preparation time: 10 minutes
Cooking time: 0 minutes
Servings: 2

Ingredients:

- 1 cup coffee drip
- 1 cup Hong-Kong style milk tea
- 1/2 – 1 cup ice cubes

Directions:

1. Mix the tea plus coffee in your medium pitcher.
2. Add the ice into your 2 glasses, pour tea coffee mix, serve and enjoy!

Nutrition: Calories: 108, Carbs: 9g, Fat: 6g, Protein: 6g

164. Italian-Style Affogato Coffee

Preparation time: 5 minutes
Cooking time: 0 minutes
Servings: 1

Ingredients:

- 1 scoop of vanilla gelato
- 2 oz espresso

For the Garnishing:

- A piece of chocolate, grated

Directions:

1. Chill your glass in your fridge for a while.
2. Add a scoop of vanilla gelato to your chilled glass, pour the coffee and garnish with grated chocolate. Serve immediately.

Nutrition: Calories: 142, Carbs: 16g, Fat: 8g, Protein: 3g

165.   Café De Olla

Preparation time: 5 minutes
Cooking time: 5 minutes
Servings: 2

Ingredients:

- 2 cups water
- 1 large stick of cinnamon
- ¼ cup Mexican coffee, coarsely ground
- 1 tbsp brown sugar

Directions:

1. Pour water in a saucepan over medium heat, add cinnamon, coffee, plus brown sugar and bring the mixture to boil. Then decrease heat and allow the mixture to simmer for 3 to 5 minutes.

2. Once ready, strain and pour into coffee mugs, serve immediately.

Nutrition: Calories: 42, Carbs: 86g, Fat: 0g, Protein: 0g

166.   Icy Jazz Berry Coffee

Preparation time: 10 minutes
Cooking time: 0 minutes
Servings: 10

Ingredients:

- 1 package (10 oz) raspberries, frozen
- ½ cup white sugar
- 10 mint sprigs
- 10 cups cold coffee
- 1 pinch half and half
- ½ cup water
- 1 cup whipped cream, sweetened
- 10 raspberries, whole

Directions:

1. Add ice cubes into 10 serving glasses and set aside. In a blender, add sugar, frozen raspberries and water, blend to make puree. In a large bowl, strain the raspberries-sugar mixture.

2. Add pinch of half and half and coffee, mix thoroughly. Pour the coffee mixture into 10 serving glasses. Serve with whipped cream, whole raspberries and mint sprigs on top.

Nutrition: Calories: 155, Carbs: 22g, Fat: 7g, Protein: 2g

167.   Mediterranean Coffee

Preparation time: 10 minutes
Cooking time: 5 minutes
Servings: 8

Ingredients:

- 8 cups strongly brewed coffee
- 4 cinnamon sticks
- ½ tsp. aniseed, tied in a cheesecloth
- lemon & orange twists for garnishing
- 1/3 cup white sugar
- ¼ cup chocolate syrup
- 1 ½ tsp. cloves, whole
- ½ cup whipped cream for garnishing

Directions:

1. In a saucepan over medium-high heat, add sugar, cinnamon sticks, freshly brewed strong coffee, chocolate syrup, aniseed and whole cloves.
2. Bring the mixture to boil, then reduce heat and allow to simmer.
3. Once ready, strain and pour into mugs, and serve with whipped cream and lemon and orange twists on top.

Nutrition: Calories: 109, Carbs: 12g, Fat: 7g, Protein: 1g

168.   Scandinavian Egg Coffee

Preparation time: 10 minutes
Cooking time: 10 minutes
Servings: 8

Ingredients:

- 4-1/2 quarts of water
- 1 egg white
- 1-1/2 cups regular grind, Scandinavian or Danish blend coffee
- ½ cup cold water

Directions:

1. In a large saucepan, pour 4 ½ quarts of water and bring to boil. In a separate bowl, mix egg white and coffee, reserve egg shell. Add egg shell and coffee-egg mixture into water and bring to boil again.
2. Once the mixture start to boil, take off from heat and let it steep for 1 to 2 minutes. To settle the ground, gradually add cold water. Once ready, transfer to the mugs and serve immediately.

169.   Costa Rican Coffee

Preparation time: 5 minutes
Cooking time: 5 minutes
Servings: 4

Ingredients:

- 2 cups cold water
- 8 tbsp finely ground Costa Rican coffee
- 1 tsp sugar

Directions:

1. In a saucepan add water. Place it over medium heat and bring it to a boil.
2. Place a coffee filteror folded cheesecloth in a stainer. Add cpffee in it and place it over a serving glass.
3. Pour hot water over the coffee and wait until it runs down and the coffee steeps.
4. Add sugar to the coffee and serve.

Nutrition: Calories: 24, Carbs: 0g, Fat: 0g, Protein: 0g

170.   Europe Coffee

Preparation time: 5 minutes
Cooking time: 0 minutes
Servings: 2

Ingredients:

- 1 egg white
- ¼ tsp vanilla extract
- 1 cup strong hot coffee (preferably dark roast)
- 2 tbsp half and half

Directions:

1. In a bowl, add vanilla and egg white, beat until stiff, then transfer equal portions to two mugs.
2. Pour coffee and a half and half on top. Serve immediately.

Nutrition: Calories: 32, Carbs: 1g, Fat: 2g, Protein: 2g

171. Black Forest Coffee

Preparation time: 5 minutes
Cooking time: 0 minutes
Servings: 1

Ingredients:

- 1 tbsp Maraschino cherry juice
- 6 oz freshly brewed hot coffee
- Whipped cream, as needed
- 2 tbsp chocolate syrup
- Maraschino cherries, as needed
- Shaved chocolate chips as needed

Directions:

1. Combine the coffee, chocolate syrup, and cherry juice in your coffee mug, and stir it well.
2. Garnish the coffee with whipped cream, then top it with some chocolate shavings plus the Maraschino cherry. Serve and enjoy!

Nutrition: Calories: 240, Carbs: 42g, Fat: 7g, Protein: 3g

172. Coffee Almond Floats

Preparation time: 5 minutes
Cooking time: 0 minutes
Servings: 2

- **Ingredients:**
- 2 tbsp coffee granules
- 1 tbsp hot water
- 2 cups 2% milk
- 2 tbsp brown sugar
- 1/8 tsp almond extract
- 1 cup vanilla ice cream

Directions:

1. Dissolve the coffee granules in a small pitcher in hot water. Add extract, brown sugar, and milk.
2. Into 2 chilled glasses, place a spoon of ice cream. Add the coffee mixture on top and serve.

Nutrition: Calories: 314, Carbohydrate: 42 g, Fat: 12 g, Protein: 11 g

173.   Paprika Infused Coffee

Preparation time: 5 minutes
Cooking time: 0 minutes
Servings: 1

Ingredients:

- ¾ cup hot brewed coffee
- ½ tsp paprika powder
- 1 tbsp heavy cream

Directions:

1. Add the brewed coffee to a serving glass and stir in the paprika powder, mix well.
2. Then add heavy cream and mix thoroughly. Serve immediately.

Nutrition: Calories 57, Fat 5.7g, Carbs 1g, Protein 0.7g

174.   Cafe Con Leche

Preparation time: 5 minutes
Cooking time: 0 minutes
Servings: 1

Ingredients:

- 1 tbsp dark roasted coffee
- ½ cup water
- ½ cup hot milk
- Sugar as per taste

Directions:

1. Brew ½ cup strong coffee from 1 tbsp dark roasted coffee, and add sugar as you like.
2. Pour coffee into your cup, add the hot milk, and serve hot.

Nutrition: Calories: 39, Carbs: 5g, Fat: 0g, Protein: 4g

175.   Peanut Butter Jelly Coffee Smoothie

Preparation time: 5 minutes
Cooking time: 0 minutes
Servings: 2

Ingredients:

- 1 cup cold, strong coffee
- 1 cup milk, 2% milkfat
- 1 tbsp peanut butter
- 4 tbsp strawberry jelly

Directions:

1. Place coffee, milk, peanut butter and strawberry jelly in a blender, and blend at high speed until foamy.
2. Once ready, pour into your glasses and serve.

Nutrition: Calories: 220, Carbs: 34g, Fat: 7g, Protein: 7g

176.   Mint Vanilla Coffee

Preparation time: 5 minutes
Cooking time: 0 minutes
Servings: 4

Ingredients:

- 1 cup cold, strong coffee
- 1 cup vanilla ice cream
- 1 cup mint ice cream
- 1 tsp mint extract
- mint leaves for garnish

Directions:

1. Place the ice creams, coffee, plus mint extract into your blender, and blend until consistent and smooth.
2. Once ready, divide and transfer to the 4 wine glasses and serve with mint leaves on top.

Nutrition: Calories: 176, Carbs: 16g, Fat: 12g, Protein: 2g

177.   Hot Coffee Masala

Preparation time: 5 minutes
Cooking time: 5 minutes
Servings: 2

Ingredients:

- 2 cups water
- 1 whole star anise pod
- 1 1/2 tsp coffee granules
- 2 tsp white sugar
- 2 cumin seeds, or to taste
- 1/2 cinnamon stick
- 2 tsp nonfat dry milk powder

Directions:

1. Boil water in a saucepan; star anise pod, add cinnamon stick, and cumin seeds, then stir. Decrease heat to a simmer; cook while occasionally stirring for 2 to 3 minutes.

2. Mix in instant coffee; let the drink simmer gently for another 2 minutes. Transfer the drink to mugs.

3. Strain out the spices, add in 1 tsp. of white sugar plus 1 tsp of nonfat dry milk powder in each mug, and stir it well. Serve and enjoy!

Nutrition: Calories: 31, Carbohydrate: 6.5 g, Fat: 0.1 g, Protein: 1.2 g

178.   Turkish Coffee

Preparation time: 5 minutes
Cooking time: 5 minutes
Servings: 5

Ingredients:

- 1 1/4 cups cold milk
- 2 1/2 tbsp finely ground Turkish-style coffee
- 5 tsp white sugar, or to taste

Directions:

1. Mix the milk, coffee, and sugar in a saucepan over medium heat until the sugar completely dissolves. Cook until the liquid begins making bubbles.

2. Leave on the stove for another 30 seconds, then remove from heat. Serve hot.

Nutrition: Calories: 48, Carbohydrate: 7.3 g, Fat: 1.2 g, Protein: 2.1 g

179.   Hot Buttered Coffee

Preparation time: 15 minutes
Cooking time: 0 minutes
Servings: 20

Ingredients:

- 1 cup brown sugar
- ½ tsp. ground cinnamon
- ¼ tsp. allspice, ground
- 1/8 tsp. cloves, ground
- ¼ cup butter, softened
- 1 tsp. vanilla extract
- ¼ tsp. nutmeg, ground

For serving:

- 1 cup hot brewed coffee (French or another dark roast)
- whipped cream & Cinnamon sticks

Directions:

1. In a small bowl, add sugar, butter, cinnamon, vanilla, allspice, nutmeg and cloves, mix thoroughly to prepare spice. You can transfer the spice to an airtight container and reserve in the fridge for 2 weeks.

For hot buttered coffee:

2. Add 1 tbsp. of your spice mixture to a mug, then mix in the coffee. Serve with cinnamon stick and whipped cream on top.

Nutrition: Calories: 67, Carbohydrate: 12 g, Fat: 2 g, Protein: 0 g

180.   Orange Mint Coffee

Preparation time: 5 minutes
Cooking time: 0 minutes
Servings: 2

Ingredients:

- 2 fresh mint sprigs
- 2 cups hot strong brewed coffee
- 2 tsp sugar
- 2 unpeeled fresh orange slices
- 1/3 cup heavy whipping cream

Directions:

1. Place a mint sprig and an orange slice in 2 coffee cups. Add hot coffee into cups.
2. Beat cream in a small bowl till it forms soft peaks. Add sugar gradually; beat till it forms stiff peaks. Serve with the coffee.

181.   Vietnamese Milk Coffee

Preparation time: 5 minutes
Cooking time: 0 minutes
Servings: 1

Ingredients:

- 2 tbsp sweetened condensed milk
- 3 1/2 tsp ground coffee with chicory
- boiling water, as needed

Directions:

1. Pour the condensed milk in your glass, and set aside for a while.
2. Steep the coffee grounds in your heatproof container with boiling water within 4 minutes.
3. Pour through your coffee filter into your prepared condensed milk glass, and stir well until blended. Serve and enjoy!

Nutrition: Calories: 125, Carbohydrate: 21.2 g, Fat: 3.3 g, Protein: 3.2 g

182.   Coffee Ice Cubes

Preparation time: 5 minutes
Cooking time: 0 minutes
Servings: 2

Ingredients:

- 2 cups of filtered water
- 4 tsp. sugar
- 4 tbsp. medium-fine grind coffee
- 1 cup boiled water

Directions:

1. Brew 4 tbsp. of coffee with 2 cups of water, and stir in the sugar until it completely dissolves.
2. Transfer the coffee to the ice cube trays, and place in the freezer for a night.
3. Add the coffee ice cubes into your cup with boiled water, and serve!

Nutrition: Calories: 70, Carbs: 17g, Fat: 0g, Protein: 0g

183. Cotton Candy Coffee

Preparation time: 5 minutes
Cooking time: 0 minutes
Servings: 1

Ingredients:

- 2 shots espresso
- ½-1 cup milk
- 1 handful of ice cubes
- 1 handful of cotton candy

Directions:

1. Pour the milk into your glass with ice cubes.
2. Shape the cotton candy to form a ball larger than your glass top. Stick a skewer in the middle of your cotton candy ball.
3. Gradually pour the hot espresso on top, mix well and serve.

Nutrition: Calories: 110, Carbs: 28g, Fat: 0g, Protein: 0g

184. Caramel Brownie Coffee

Preparation time: 5 minutes
Cooking time: 0 minutes
Servings: 1

Ingredients:

- 1 cup coffee brew
- 2 tbsp milk chocolate chip morsels
- 1 can whip cream
- 1 tbsp. French vanilla creamer
- 1 crumbled chocolate brownie

Directions:

1. Pour the coffee into your mug, then add the chocolate chips and mix until melted.
2. Add the creamer, stir it well, and top with whipped cream. Garnish with chocolate brownie and serve.

Nutrition: Calories: 202, Carbs: 29g, Fat: 0g, Protein: 0g

185. Fig Lavender Cold Brew Coffee

Preparation time: 5 minutes
Cooking time: 0 minutes
Servings: 1

Ingredients:

For the lavender fig syrup:

- 1 cup water
- 4 tbsp. lavender
- 1 cup sugar
- 4 fresh sliced figs

For the lavender fig coffee:

- 1 cup cold brew coffee
- 2 tbsp. cream
- 1 tbsp. lavender fig syrup
- 1 handful ice

Directions:

1. Add water, lavender, sugar and sliced figs in your saucepan, and let it simmer until sugar dissolves. Let it sit and infuse within 30 minutes before straining it into your bowl.

2. Add all the lavender fig coffee fixings into your glass with ice and stir it well. Serve and enjoy!

Nutrition: Calories: 90, Carbs: 0g, Fat: 11g, Protein: 0g

Coffee Desserts

186. Café Coffee Cookies

Preparation time: 15 minutes
Cooking time: 15 minutes
Servings: 15 cookies

Ingredients:

- ½ cup brown sugar
- ½ cup butter
- ½ cup white sugar grains
- 2 cups chocolate pieces
- 1 egg
- ½ tbsp. baking soda
- ½ cup coarsely ground pecans
- 1 ½ cups all-purpose flour
- 2 tbsp. instant coffee
- ½ cup powdered white sugar
- ¼ cup water
- Salt to taste

Directions:

1. Prepare the oven and preheat to 350 F.
2. In a mixer bowl, add eggs, butter, brown and brown sugar, mix thoroughly.
3. Stir in baking soda, 1 tbsp. instant coffee, pecans, salt, flour, and chocolate chunks until it gets dough shape.
4. Now take a cookie sheet and place dough about ¼ cup at one-inch intervals—Bake within 15 minutes. Allow cooling at room temperature.
5. Now make a thin coffee drizzle by dissolving a teaspoon of coffee in water and stirring in sugar.
6. Drizzle the cookies with coffee drizzle, and enjoy delicious coffee cookies.

Nutrition: Calories: 296, Protein: 3.59g, Fat: 9.77g, Carbohydrates: 48.88g

187.   Coffee Rice Pudding

Preparation time: 15 minutes
Cooking time: 5 minutes
Servings: 2

Ingredients:

- 1 tbsp coffee granules
- 2 cups whole milk
- ½ cup sugar
- ¾ cup heavy cream
- ½ orange juice and zest
- ½ cup arborio rice
- 1 tsp. vanilla extract
- 2 tbsp. butter

Directions:

1. Pour orange juice, coffee and a cup of water in a large pan. Bring the mixture to boil. As soon as the mixture starts to boil, take off from the heat immediately. Then add rice to the mixture and leave there for 3 to 5 minutes.

2. Put the pan back on the stove over low heat, add vanilla and milk, and continue cooking until the rice is just cooked.

3. Remove the pan from heat. Add sugar, butter, cream, rum and orange zest. Mix well. Serve.

Nutrition: Calories: 340, Carbs: 72g, Fat: 2g, Protein: 7g

188.   Coffee Cakes

Preparation time: 15 minutes
Cooking time: 20 minutes
Servings: 16

Ingredients:

- 5 oz golden caster sugar
- 5 oz rising flour
- 1 tbsp water
- Coffee beans for garnishing
- 5 oz butter
- 4 eggs
- 2 tbsp espresso
-

For the Icing:

- 7 oz butter
- 2 tbsp. espresso and water mixture
- 7 oz. icing sugar
- 2 oz. melted chocolate

Directions:

1. Prepare the oven and preheat to 340 F.
2. In a small bowl, mix sugar with butter to form a light paste. Stir in flour, eggs, and 2 tbsp. of espresso and water mixture one by one to form a dough.
3. Take cake cases and put the dough in them with a spoon. Bake in the oven for 20 minutes, then cool at room temperature.
4. In another bowl, add icing sugar and butter, beat thoroughly. Then add, chocolate first and then add espresso while continue beating.
5. Squeeze the icing on top of every cooled cake. Drop chocolate for garnishing.

Nutrition: Calories: 283, Protein: 3.85 g, Fat: 20.52 g, Carbohydrates: 21.58 g

189. Coffee Nutella Swirl Ice Cream

Preparation time: 10 minutes + chilling time
Cooking time: 0 minutes
Servings: 2

Ingredients:

- 1 cup Nutella
- 1 tbsp. coffee granules
- 1/3 cup hot water
- 2 cups condensed sweet milk
- 14 oz. cool whipped cream

Directions:

1. Mix the hot water plus coffee granules in your mug, and let cool to room temperature.
2. In a large bowl, add cool whipped cream and condensed sweet milk with the coffee mixture.
3. In an oven-proof bowl, add a spoonful of Nutella and transfer to the oven, heat for a few seconds until melts. Pour into the large bowl mixture by swirling and avoiding complete mixing.
4. Once ready, transfer to the freezer and leave for four to five hours. Serve in small ice cream bowls.

Nutrition: Calories: 268, Protein: 2 g, Fat: 17 g, Carbohydrates: 26 g

190.   Espresso Panna Cotta

Preparation time: 10 minutes + chilling time - **Cooking time:** 5 minutes
Servings: 4

Ingredients:

- 2g gelatin crystals
- ½ cup sugar
- 1 oz. espresso
- 12 oz. heavy cream
- 1 tsp. vanilla extract

Directions:

1. Pour in sugar and cream in a small pan and gently simmer while stirring irregularly.

2. Add espresso in the same pan and stir to mix.

3. Then remove from the heat instantly, add gelatin and stir until combined completely.

4. Divide the mixture into small bowls and transfer to the fridge, leave for 4 to 6 hours until panna cotta sets. Serve immediately and enjoy!

191.   Coffee Mousse

Preparation time: 10 minutes + chilling time - **Cooking time:** 10 minutes
Servings: 4

Ingredients:

- ½ cup water
- 1 ½ cup heavy cream
- 5 tbsp. powdered sugar
- pure cocoa powder, garnish
- ½ cup white sugar
- 3 1/3 tbsp coffee granules
- 4 egg yolks

Directions:

1. Add sugar, water, plus coffee granules to your small pot and combine.

2. Place the pot over medium heat and bring to boil while stirring intermittently. Once coffee reaches syrupy consistency, remove the pot from heat.

3. Add egg yolks in a large bowl and beat while gradually adding the coffee and continue beating for 3 to 5 minutes. Set aside.

4. Add heavy cream and powdered sugar in another bowl, whisk thoroughly until fluffy.

5. Gently fold the prepared coffee mixture into fluffy heavy cream using rubber spatula.

6. Transfer the mousse into a large bowl, put in the freezer, and let chill for 10 to 12 hours. Once done, remove from freezer and serve immediately.

192. Espresso Hazelnuts Balls

Preparation time: 15 minutes
Cooking time: 0 minutes
Servings: 3

Ingredients:

- 1 package (9 oz.) of chocolate wafers
- 1 tbsp. espresso
- 2 ½ tbsp. light corn syrup
- ½ cup sugar
- 1 cup hazelnuts, skinned and toasted
- 1 ½ cups powdered sugar
- ½ cup orange liqueur

Directions:

1. In a food processor, crush hazelnuts plus wafers, then add the powdered sugar and mix thoroughly, remove and set aside.
2. In the same food processor, add espresso, orange liqueur, corn syrup and wafer crumbs, blend until mixture becomes pasty.
3. Divide the mixture into equal portions and transform them into ball shape, set aside.
4. Add sugar in a separate bowl. Dredge the balls in the sugar and roll to coat evenly. Arrange in the baking sheet lined with parchment paper and place in the refrigerator to age, then serve.

Nutrition: Calories: 160, Carbs: 12g, Fat: 13g, Protein: 3g

193. Plain Coffee Ice Cream

Preparation time: 10 minutes + chilling time
Cooking time: 0 minutes
Servings: 3

Ingredients:

- 10 oz heavy cream
- 6 oz. condensed milk
- 2 tbsp. coffee liqueur
- 2 tbsp. espresso

Directions:

1. Take a large bowl and put all ingredients in it. Whisk all the ingredients until mixture becomes airy.
2. Cover the bowl with wrapping plastic and leave overnight in the freezer. Serve in ice cream cups.

Nutrition: Calories: 362, Protein: 3.75 g, Fat: 36.84 g, Carbohydrates: 5.51 g

194.   Coffee Brownies

Preparation time: 15 minutes
Cooking time: 30 minutes
Servings: 6

Ingredients:

- 1 cup all-purpose flour
- 1 pinch of baking powder
- 2 ½ tbsp. coffee granules
- 3 eggs
- Salt to taste
- 2 oz. butter
- 1-oz chocolate
- 1 tsp. vanilla
- 3 tbsp. sugar
- ¾ cup mashed walnuts

Directions:

1. Prepare the oven and preheat to 380 F.
2. In a bowl, mix baking powder, flour, coffee plus salt. In another oven-safe bowl, add butter and chocolate, transfer to the oven and heat until melts.
3. Add sugar and eggs to the melted mixture and stir well until fluffy. Then add walnuts and vanilla. Combine both mixtures in a greased saucepan.
4. Bake for 20 to 30 minutes. Then remove from heat, allow to cool and cut into equal sized squares using a sharp knife, serve immediately.

Nutrition: Calories: 309, Protein: 8.49 g, Fat: 19.27 g, Carbohydrates: 25.99 g

Preparation time: 15 minutes
Cooking time: 10-12 minutes
Servings: 34 cookies

Ingredients:

- ¾ cup granulated sugar
- 1 cup of shortening
- 2 eggs
- ½ cup brown sugar
- 1 tbsp. coffee granules
- 2 tbsp. milk
- 2 1/3 cups plain flour
- 1 tsp. vanilla extract
- 1 tsp. baking soda
- 2 tbsp. cocoa powder
- 1 cup pecans, chopped
- ½ tsp. salt
- ¾ cup raisins
- 1 cup semisweet chocolate chips
- ¾ cup flaked coconut

Directions:

1. Prepare the oven and preheat to 375 F.
2. In a large bowl, add both sugars and shortening, beat until fluffy.
3. Then add milk, eggs, vanilla and coffee granules, combine thoroughly.
4. Sift cocoa, flour, salt and baking soda in a large bowl.
5. Then add raisins, pecans and chocolate chips, combine thoroughly.
6. Line tray with parchment paper, place 2 scoops of cookie batter onto the baking tray, and make sure each cookie is 2" apart.
7. Transfer the tray to the preheated oven and bake for 10 to 12 minutes until golden brown. Once done, remove from oven, let it cool for 5 to 10 minutes, and then serve.

Nutrition: Calories: 145, Carbs: 18g, Fat: 7g, Protein: 1g

196.   Creamy Coffee Pie

Preparation time: 15 minutes + chilling time
Cooking time: 20-30 minutes
Servings: 8

Ingredients:

- 1 puff pastry
- 3 cups coffee ice cream
- ¼ cup hot fudge ice cream topping
- ¼ cup cold milk
- 6 oz. instant chocolate pudding mix
- 1 cup marshmallow cream
- 1 ¾ cup whipped cream
- ¼ cup semisweet chocolate chips, topping

Directions:

1. Prepare the oven and preheat to 390 F.
2. Fit puff pastry in a 9" pan and cut the extra pastry.
3. Make small hole in the puff pastry using fork, transfer to the preheated oven and bake for 25 to 30 minutes, then remove. Allow to cool completely.
4. Pour hot fudge topping over the puff pastry. Set aside.
5. Add pudding mix, ice cream, coffee and milk in a bowl and mix well.
6. Mix marshmallow cream and whipped cream in another bowl. Pour the mixture over the pie and spread evenly using a spatula.
7. Garnish with chocolate chips. Cover using cling film, and place in a freezer 6 to 8 hours. Serve and enjoy!

Nutrition: Calories: 270, Carbs: 23g, Fat: 2g, Protein: 0g

197.   Coffee Fig Dip

Preparation time: 10 minutes
Cooking time: 5 minutes
Servings: 1-2 cups

Ingredients:

- 4 figs, chopped
- 1 cup white wine
- ½ tsp. ground coffee
- 2 tbsp. double cream
- Pinch of black pepper
- 1 shallot, chopped
- 1 tbsp. green tea
- 1 tsp. tarragon leaves
- Salt to taste

Directions:

1. Pour oil in a pan over medium heat, add shallots and sauté for a minute or two. Pour in white wine and bring the mixture to a boil for 2 to 3 minutes.

2. Now add green tea and ground coffee, mix thoroughly.

3. In a blender, add the fig mixture in the pan. Then add tarragon, cream, black pepper and salt. Blend until consistent. Serve!

Nutrition: Calories: 37, Carbs: 10g, Fat: 0g, Protein: 0g

198.   Espresso Truffles

Preparation time: 15 minutes
Cooking time: 3 minutes
Servings: 46 truffles

Ingredients:

- 1 cup cream
- 1 tsp. instant espresso
- 8 oz. bittersweet chocolate chips
- 8 oz. semisweet chocolate chips
- 1 tbsp. vanilla extract
- 1 oz. cocoa powder

Directions:

1. Heat espresso and cream in a pan on medium heat for three minutes. Remove from heat and add bittersweet chocolate, semisweet, and vanilla extract; mix well.

2. Put this mixture in your bowl and refrigerate for 4 hours. When cooled, take a scoop and pull out small one" diameter balls. Roll these in cocoa powder and enjoy.

Nutrition: Calories: 61, Protein: 0.7 g, Fat: 3.72 g, Carbohydrates: 7.05 g

199. Eggless Buttermilk Coffee Cake

Preparation time: 15 minutes
Cooking time: 30 minutes
Servings: 9

Ingredients:

- non-stick cooking spray
- 2 cups all-purpose flour
- 2 cups brown sugar, packed
- 1 tsp. baking soda
- ½ cup butter
- 1 cup buttermilk or sour milk
- ½ tsp. salt

Directions:

1. Prepare the oven and preheat to 350 F. Prepare 9x9x2 inch square baking pan by greasing it with cooking spray.
2. In a medium-sized mixing bowl, mix the flour, sugar, and butter until it has the consistency of fine crumbs.
3. Remove and reserve ½ cup of the mixture for the topping. Add salt, baking soda, and buttermilk to the remaining flour mixture. Blend well. Spread into prepared pan.
4. Sprinkle the reserved crumbs over your cake.
5. Transfer to the preheated oven and bake for 30 to 40 minutes until an inserted toothpick comes out clean from the center. Be careful about the brown sugar topping as it burns easily.

Nutrition: Calories: 383, Protein: 4g, Fat: 1g, Carbohydrates: 70g

200. Tiramisu Dip

Preparation time: 15 minutes
Cooking time: 0 minutes
Servings: 3 cups

Ingredients:

- 1 cup cold heavy cream
- ¾ cups + 1 tbsp. powdered sugar
- 1 tsp. vanilla extract
- 8 oz. mascarpone cheese, room temp.
- ½ cup brewed coffee, chilled
- 1 oz. semisweet chocolate

Directions:

1. Add 1 tbsp. of the powdered sugar cream in your mixing bowl, beat until you get stiff peaks. Set aside.
2. Add remaining powdered sugar and mascarpone in another bowl, mix well until consistent. Then add the coffee and vanilla, mix again until well blended.
3. Add grated chocolate to the mixture. Then add the whipped cream and using a spatula gently fold into the mascarpone mixture.
4. Serve with remaining grated chocolate on top.

Nutrition: Calories: 35, Carbs: 6g, Fat: 2g, Protein: 1g

201. Maple Mocha Popsicles

Preparation time: 15 minutes + chilling time
Cooking time: 0 minutes
Servings: 12

Ingredients:

- ½ cup half and half
- ¼ cup chocolate syrup
- 1 tbsp. coffee granules
- 2 cups heavy whipping cream
- ¼ cup maple syrup
-

Directions:

1. In a large bowl, add half and half, cream, maple syrup, chocolate syrup, and instant coffee. Whisk thoroughly.
2. Transfer the mixture to the molds and insert popsicle sticks.
3. Poke a hole in the middle of the foil so that the stick does not move. Transfer to the freezer for a day, then remove and serve.

Nutrition: Calories: 316, Carbs: 29g, Fat: 20g, Protein: 4g

Made in United States
North Haven, CT
09 January 2023